THE COFFINS OF THE PRIESTS OF AMUN

Sidestone Press

THE COFFINS OF THE PRIESTS OF AMUN

Egyptian coffins from the 21st Dynasty in the collection
of the National Museum of Antiquities in Leiden

edited by
Lara Weiss

PAPERS ON ARCHAEOLOGY OF THE
LEIDEN MUSEUM OF ANTIQUITIES

© 2018 Rijksmuseum van Oudheden; The individual authors

PALMA: Papers on Archaeology of the Leiden Museum of Antiquities (volume 17)

Published by Sidestone Press, Leiden
www.sidestone.com

Imprint: Sidestone Press

Lay-out & cover design: Sidestone Press
Photograph cover:
Anonymous coffin, Thebes, *Bab el-Gasus*, 22ᵉ Dynasty (?)
(ca. 950-900 BCE), in the Dutch National Museum of Antiquities,
photo: Karsten Wentink

ISBN 978-90-8890-492-9 (softcover)
ISBN 978-90-8890-493-6 (hardcover)
ISBN 978-90-8890-494-3 (PDF e-book)

ISSN 2034-550X

Contents

Preface	**7**
Lara Weiss	
1 The Vatican Coffin Project	**9**
Alessia Amenta, Christian Greco, Ulderico Santamaria, and Lara Weiss	
2 The 21st Dynasty: The Theocracy of Amun, and the Position of the Theban Priestly Families	**13**
Gerard P.F. Broekman	
3 The Tomb of the Priests of Amun at Thebes: The History of the Find	**21**
Rogério Sousa	
4 The Coffins in Leiden	**35**
Liliane Mann, Christian Greco, and Lara Weiss	
5 Painting Techniques of the Leiden Coffins	**49**
Elsbeth Geldhof	
6 Coffin Reuse in the 21st Dynasty: A Case Study of the Coffins in the *Rijksmuseum van Oudheden*	**69**
Kathlyn M. Cooney	
Bibliography	**97**

Preface

Lara Weiss

The National Museum of Antiquities (in the following *Rijksmuseum van Oudheden*) in Leiden joined the Vatican Coffin Project in 2011. The cooperation and team spirit in this international and also interdisciplinary team (see chapter 1) has been a great experience for me during the past two years and I am delighted to be able to pursue this cooperation initiated by my friend and colleague Christian Greco. I would like to thank especially Alessia Amenta and Giovanna Prestipino, as well as Ulderico Santamaria of the *Musei Vaticani* to welcome me and our new restorer Helbertijn Krudop in the Vatican Coffin Project team. Needless to say that also the cooperation with our partners from Turin and Paris is a very fruitful and pleasant one! As a newcomer to the *Rijksmuseum van Oudheden* in Leiden, I was asked to take over responsibility to publish the results of the initial phase of the project conducted by Christian Greco, Elsbeth Geldhof, and Liliane Mann. I arrived in Leiden in 2014, i.e. after the end of regular work on what we now call the first phase of the Leiden contribution to the Vatican Coffin Project, but it has fallen to me to put it into a state in which it can be made available to a wider public. Those involved in the project have entrusted me with their working materials, notes, and protocols, on the basis of which we have been able to edit their articles which form the basis of this book. Although I have enjoyed close contact with the members of the project, it has not always been possible to answer all questions so there may be lacunae in the presentation of the material. I am grateful for the input of all members of the project and their trust, and I am sure that the most valuable and significant results are here made available in the best possible way. I would also like to thank Gerard Broekman and Rogério Sousa for providing the historical frame of the project, as well as Kathlyn Cooney for adding her work on the reuse of the Leiden coffins.

Leiden, May 2017

Chapter 1

The Vatican Coffin Project

Alessia Amenta, Christian Greco,

Ulderico Santamaria, and Lara Weiss

1.1 Introduction

The ancient Egyptians believed that only an intact body was eligible to survive in the afterlife.[1] Coffins protected the mummy in his/her tomb and therefore played an important role for fulfilling the requirements of reaching the ancient Egyptian afterlife. This coffin provided physical protection in form of a (usually) wooden shelter around the corpse, but also a magical guard. Apotropaic figures of gods and religious spells protected the mummy in the realm of the deceased. Also not unimportant, coffins were commodities that were manufactured and traded, and inform us about the socio-historical background of their owners.[2] In spite of this important role of coffins in the ancient Egyptian culture, coffin studies remain a rather marginal field of study in Egyptology. Of course the so-called Coffin Texts have been in the centre of attention from the early days of Egyptology,[3] and interesting work has been done on iconography and style of, for example, the colourful Third Intermediate Period coffins.[4] However, an approach that takes seriously the materiality of Egyptian coffins, i.e. not study them as bearers of text/decoration or mummy containers only, is a *desideratum* in Egyptology. The Vatican Coffin Project seeks to close this gap by focussing in particular on the material aspects of the Egyptian coffins together with their symbolic and cultural values.[5]

---

1   Compare, for example, J.H. Taylor, *Mummies. Death and the Afterlife in Ancient Egypt. Treasures from the British Museum*, Santa Ana 2005.
2   E.g. K.M. Cooney, *The Cost of the Death, The Social and Economic Value of Ancient Egyptian Funerary Art in the Ramesside Period*, Leiden 2007 and see chapter 6.
3   E.g. A. De Buck, *The Egyptian Coffin Texts*, Chicago 1935.
4   Notably A. Niwiński, *21st Dynasty Coffins from Thebes: Chronological and Typological Studies*, Mainz 1988 and R. van Walsem, *The Coffin of Djedmonthuiufankh in the National Museum of Antiquities at Leiden*, Leiden 1997.
5   See also A. Amenta, 'The Vatican Coffin Project', in: E. Pischikova, J. Budka and K. Griffin (eds), *Thebes in the First Millennium BC*, Cambridge 2014, pp. 483-499.

1.2 Partners and Aims of the Vatican Coffin Project

The international research cooperation was set up in 2008 between the Department of Ancient Egyptian Antiquities of the *Musei Vaticani*, directed by Alessia Amenta, and the Diagnostic Laboratory for Conservation of the *Musei Vaticani*, directed by Ulderico Santamaria, and currently involves the following institutions:[6]

- *Musei Vaticani*, Vatican City State
- *Musée du Louvre*, Paris
- *Rijksmuseum van Oudheden*, Leiden
- *Museo Egizio*, Turin
- *Centre de Recherche et de Restauration des Musées de France*, Paris
- *Centro Conservazione e Restauro 'La Venaria Reale'*, Turin
- Victoria Asensi Amoros, Xylodata Paris

All these institutions are sharing the same approach for research and conservation of anthropoid wooden 'yellow' coffins dating to the 21st Dynasty (1076-944 BCE) till the begin of the 22nd Dynasty (ca. 943-870 BCE). These coffins are characteristic for their 'yellow' background. The final goal of the Vatican Coffin Project is to create a shared database with all the information concerning construction and painting techniques, conservation methodology, and scientific analyses.

In Leiden, Christian Greco chose a group of 'yellow' coffins found in the *Bab el-Gasus* cache (see chapter 3) as a starting point.[7] The choice for the *Bab el-Gasus* group was based on their shared provenance: the coffins were made for a known community in a known period of time, namely the priests of Amun living in the 21st Dynasty (1076-944 BCE) (see chapter 2 and chapter 6).[8]

1.3 Interdisciplinary approach

Apart from its novel research question, the strength and innovation of the Vatican Coffin Project lie in its interdisciplinary approach. The project's aim is to scrutinise the coffins as closely as possible, which produces a mass of data requiring the combination of different skills and competences. Therefore the Vatican Coffin Project is organised in three working groups: Egyptology, Diagnostic (i.e. scientific analyses applied to coffins) and Conservation. By sharing knowledge and technologies the curators, scientists and conservators from the participating institutions are able to study 'their' coffins from all three perspectives. This unique cooperation between museums and restoration laboratories thus allows a full analysis of the coffins. The manufacture and painting techniques used by the ancient Egyptians will be studied as well as the coffins' iconography and style, the prosopography and titles of the coffin owners (the *Bab el-Gasus* community in the case

---

6   In addition to the institutions, professor Kathlyn M. Cooney (UCLA University) is collaborating in the project for the study of the 're-use' of 21st Dynasty coffins.

7   The same applies to the ongoing study of the Vatican Coffin Project in the Vatican Museums, but not in the Louvre Museum and the *Museo Egizio* in Turin, museum collections that study 'yellow' coffins dating to the 21st to 22nd Dynasties, which are not provenanced from *Bab el-Gasus* cache.

8   The Vatican Museums and the *Rijksmuseum van Oudheden* in Leiden received coffins from *Bab el-Gasus* in 1893; Lot XVII went to the Vatican (Inv. nos. MV 25015, 25035, 25016, 51515, 25021, 25020, 25022) and Lot XI to the *Rijksmuseum van Oudheden* (Leiden inv. nos. F 93/10.1, F 93/10.2, F 93/10.3, and F 93/10.4). Neither the *Musée du Louvre* nor the *Museo Egizio* have coffins from this cache, however, and they have begun the project with the study and analyses of other 'yellow coffins' of the 21st Dynasty: see H. Guichard, S. Pages-Camagna, and N. Timbart, 'The coffin of Tanetchedmut of the Musée du Louvre: First study and restoration for the Vatican Coffin Project', in: A. Amenta and H. Guichard (eds), *Proceedings of the First Vatican Coffin Conference (Vatican Museums, 19-22 June 2013)* (Rome 2017, pp. 169-178); A. Amenta, 'The restoration of the coffin of Butehamon. New points for reflection from scientific investigations', in *Proceedings of the Conference Ancient Egyptian Coffins. Past-Present-Future* (Cambridge, 7-9 April 2016), (in press).

of Leiden), the religious meaning of the coffins, etc. One overarching question of the project is to identify the workshops where the coffins were made and how the workshops were organised. In spite of their shared provenance (*Bab el-Gasus*), the place where the coffins were made is still unclear. It is the fact that all these coffins were owned by a group of Amun priests (see chapter 2), as well as the coffins' similar decoration that had sparked the idea that the coffins might have been crafted in connected workshops using similar techniques. For example, the coffins are recognisable because they are 'yellow' and display characteristic motifs and a rich decoration typical for the beginning of the First Millennium BCE.

Another important research aspect of the project is the more recent history of the coffins. Prior to their discovery, the coffins were protected in the stable microclimate of the tomb in case of the Leiden coffins for about 3000 years in the *Bab el-Gasus* cache (see chapter 3). Protected by the more or less constant temperature and low relative humidity the coffins survived the centuries in a quite good condition. However, the micro-climate suddenly changed when the Leiden coffins were excavated in the 19th century, and again; when they were transported from *Bab el-Gasus* to Cairo in a steamer. Subsequent shipping to and arrival in Europe brought the coffins to yet another dramatically different climate. The coffins thus underwent a considerable amount of handling, packaging and transport before arriving in Europe almost two years after their excavation (see chapter 3). All this caused damage to the coffins such as warped wood, delamination of paint layers, and bio-deterioration. Whether conservation measures were taken in Cairo after the excavation of the coffins remains unclear. In the Leiden museum archive, for example, we find evidence that conservation was performed after the arrival of the coffins in Leiden (see below chapter 4). What exactly was done, however, has not been recorded. In the Vatican Coffin Project therefore there is a particular attention also to recognise previous treatments of the coffins and to test and share new methods of conservation. For example, the Diagnostic Laboratory of the *Musei Vaticani*, in collaboration with the conservator Giovanna Prestipino, have carried out a series of experiments on adhesives and consolidating materials and established a conservation record wherein the most effective conservation approaches. In addition the most suitable materials to be used on polychrome wooden objects are collected.[9]

1.4 Preliminary Results

Four years ago, the *First Vatican Coffin Conference* (held in the *Musei Vaticani* from 19-22th June 2013) opened the debate on the different subjects relating to the study of coffins.[10] The conference, organised by the *Musei Vaticani*, in collaboration with the *Musée du Louvre* and the *Rijksmuseum van Oudheden* in Leiden, once again stressed the importance of a comprehensive interdisciplinary study of coffins as commodities in a social-historic context and not just as bearers of text and iconography. An exhibition (20 April-15 September 2013) was held under the curatorship of Christian Greco in the *Rijksmuseum van Oudheden*, which presented the find of the *Bab el-Gasus* coffins as an archaeological event, but also focussed on the conservation of these coffins. Many *Bab el-Gasus* coffins were in poor condition. The paint delaminated and the coffins were dusty. The Vatican Coffin Project and its joint expertise allowed investigation and restoration of the coffins using the most modern techniques. During the Leiden exhibition conservator Elsbeth Geldhof – employed especially for that project – continued her restoration work publicly, thereby also answering questions from visitors (on her findings see chapter 5). The present book presents the first results of the studies related to the Leiden coffins that

---

9 G. Prestipino, U. Santamaria, F. Morresi, *et al.*, 'Sperimentazione di adesivi e consolidanti per il restauro di manufatti lignei policromi egizi', in: *Lo Stato dell'Arte 13. Atti del XIII Congresso Nazionale IGIIC (Torino, 22-24 ottobre 205)*, Turin 2015, pp. 261-270.

10 Cf. A. Amenta and H. Guichard (eds), *Proceedings of the First Vatican Coffin Conference*, Rome 2017.

were carried out in cooperation with the Diagnostic Laboratory of the *Musei Vaticani* and the *Rijksdienst voor Cultureel Erfgoed* (RCE, Cultural Heritage Agency of the Netherlands). Also the book is meant as a first introduction to the Vatican Coffin Project and to contextualise the coffins in their historical time period (see chapter 2). Their find in Egypt in 1892 will be discussed (chapter 3) as well as their journey to Leiden (chapter 4). In the final chapter, Kathlyn Cooney presents her research on the reuse of the coffins (chapter 6). We would like to thank restorer Giovanna Prestipino from the Diagnostic Laboratory of the *Musei Vaticani* as well as all the authors for their patience and willingness to contribute to this volume. Robbert Jan Looman kindly created the figures for chapter 4. Last but not least we would like to thank Pieter ter Keurs for his support and for including the book to the Leiden PALMA series and Karsten Wentink and Corné van Woerdekom for the pleasant editing process.

Chapter 2

The 21st Dynasty: The Theocracy of Amun, and the Position of the Theban Priestly Families

Gerard P.F. Broekman

2.1 Introduction

The most conspicuous characteristic of the 21st Egyptian Dynasty is its administrative bifurcation, the border between the northern and southern parts of the country being located in the region of Herakleopolis Magna. Though extant contemporaneous monuments do not give any direct indication as to the reason for the partition of Egypt, it may be explained from the nature of the Libyan rule, which, as Karl Jansen-Winkeln has shown, began with the accession of the 21st Dynasty.[11]

In fact this meant the end of Egypt as a unitary state, that had existed – with a few interruptions – for about two millennia, in which there was according to the Egyptian religious-political tradition only one unique ruler, the *King of Upper- and Lower Egypt*.

Under the kings of the 18th and 19th Dynasties (1539-1191 BCE) Egypt was an imperial power with the god Amun as the chief deity of the Egyptian empire. The kings of these dynasties used to attribute all their successful enterprises to Amun, and they donated much of their wealth and captured spoil for the construction and decoration of temples dedicated to him, resulting in an increasing influence of the priests of Amun, not in the least the High Priest. During the 20th Dynasty royal authority gradually weakened, as is reflected in a letter from Piankh, High Priest and General under the last king of the Dynasty Ramesses XI: *And to whom is Pharaoh – may he live, prosper, be healthy – superior still?*

With regard to the biographical and genealogical information about the Theban Priests of Amun in the 21st Dynasty we are almost completely dependent on funeral equipments – coffins, mummy braces and bandages, funerary stelae and funerary papyri – as private statues are almost completely lacking in this period. Fortunately we have at

---

11   K. Jansen-Winkeln, 'Der Beginn der Libyschen Herrschaft in Ägypten', *Biblische Notizen* 71 (1994), pp. 78-97; K. Jansen-Winkeln, 'Gab es in der altägyptischen Geschichte eine feudalistische Epoche?', *Die Welt des Orients* 30 (1999), pp. 7-20; K. Jansen-Winkeln, 'Die Fremdherrschaften in Ägypten im 1. Jahrtausend v. Chr.', *Orientalia* 69 (2000), pp. 1-20; K. Jansen-Winkeln, 'Der thebanische "Gottesstaat"', *Orientalia* 70 (2001), pp. 153-182.

our disposal 153 mummy-ensembles of priests of Amun and their families, found in the *Bab el-Gasus* in the Asasif on the west bank of the Nile at Thebes.[12]

2.2 A Chronology for the 21st Dynasty

Ascertaining a reliable chronology for the 21st Dynasty is hampered by the fact that, though many dates are preserved, most of them do not refer to a specific ruler. It is not clear either whether those dates, most of which are from Thebes, were related to the Lower-Egyptian kings or to the rulers of Upper Egypt. In the first half of the Dynasty the High Priests of Amun in Thebes have royal attributes and titles, whereas the Lower-Egyptian kings are virtually not recorded at all in Upper Egypt. In the second half, however, some Lower-Egyptian kings are well documented in Thebes, whereas the contemporary Theban High Priest of Amun Pinudjem II did not assume any royal attributes or titles. From this Jansen-Winkeln presumes that "the HP (High Priests) who called themselves kings counted their own years of reign whereas during the second half of the Dynasty the dates refer to the LE (Lower-Egyptian) kings".[13] In accordance with Jansen-Winkeln's view the following chronological table for the 21st Dynasty may be presented:[14]

Lower-Egyptian Kings		Theban High Priests	
Smendes I	1070 – 1045	Herihor	1070 – 1065
Amenemnisut	1044 – 1041	Pinudjem I	1064 – 1039
Psusennes I	1040 – 992	Menkheperre A	1038 – 990
Amenemope	991 – 983		
Osochor (Osorkon the elder)	982 – 977	Pinudjem II	989 – 966
Siamun	976 – 958	Psusennes III	965 – 957
Psusennes II	957 – 944	Psusennes II/III	956 – 944

Table 1: The Chronology of the 21st Dynasty.

Family-ties existed between some Theban High Priests and the Lower-Egyptian kings: possibly Smendes I was the father-in-law of Pinudjem I, the latter being Psusennes I's father, and Psusennes II might have been the son of the Theban High Priest Pinudjem II. The family relations of Amenemope and Siamun are unknown, whereas Osochor (Osorkon the elder) was to all probability an uncle of the founder of the 22nd Dynasty Shoshenq I.[15]

The Libyan character of the 21st Dynasty is clearly reflected in the *Report of Wenamun*. This account of the journey to Byblos by the Elder of the Portal of the temple of Amun-Re, king of the gods, Wenamun, by order of Herihor, High Priest of Amun in Thebes, presents a curious political situation in Egypt: no reference is made to any named pharaoh, and the only rulers of Egypt mentioned are Herihor residing in Thebes and Smendes and Tentamun in Tanis. Wenamun departs from Thebes in year 5 of an unnamed king on IV šmw 16, to procure timber for the construction of a new bark of Amun. At his arrival in Tanis he is hosted by Smendes and Tentamun, and they assign him to a ship bound for Phoenicia. He calls at the port of Dor, where the gold and silver, destined for the purchase of the timber, are stolen. Wenamun appeals for help to the prince of Dor regarding the stolen gold and silver, stating: "It belongs to Amun-Re, king of the gods, the lord of the lands. It belongs to Nesubanebdjed (Smendes). It belongs to

---

12 G. Daressy, 'Cercueils des prêtres d'Amon (Deuxième Trouvaille de Deir el Bahari)', *Annales du Service des Antiquités de l'Égypte* 8 (1907), pp. 3-38.
13 K. Jansen-Winkeln, 'Relative Chronology of Dyn. 21', in: E. Hornung *et al.* (eds), *Ancient Egyptian Chronology*, Leiden and Boston 2006, p. 229.
14 See Jansen-Winkeln, Relative Chronology, pp. 218-234. It should be noticed that the High Priests Masaharta, Djedkhjonsefankh and Smendes II are not included in the table of Theban High Priests, as they are chronologically of no interest.
15 J. Yoyotte, 'Un Pharaon Oublié?', *Bulletin de la Société française d'Égyptologie* 77-78 (1976/77), pp. 39-54.

Herihor, my lord, and the other great ones of Egypt (*n3 kth ꜥ3.w n kmt*)". As Arno Egberts rightly observed, the use of *kth* ('other'), suggests that Smendes and Herihor were likewise *great ones* rather than *kings*.[16] Egberts argued that in Wenamun's time "the role of pharaoh had been assigned to Amun" and that, consequently, "there was no employment for a human king anymore". Egberts further pointed out that Wenamun mentioning Khaemwaset – in all probability identical with Ramesses XI, who bore the epithet Khaemwaset – was apparently retrospective, which indicates that Khaemwaset alias Ramesses XI was dead at the time of Wenamun's voyage.[17]

Whereas such a political situation is absolutely inconceivable in terms of the Egyptian religious-political tradition, it perfectly fits the social hierarchy characteristic of Libyan tribal society, its political structure being a loose confederation reinforced by family alliances and appointments, in which tribal units were led by *chiefs* or *great chiefs*, whereas there was no need for any overarching authority.[18] Under such a political structure we may expect to find Smendes, Herihor, and the other great ones being the factual rulers of Egypt, preferring their own tribal titles to Egyptian ones and for whom "King of Upper and Lower Egypt was simply a title".[19] Consequently, in their conception there was no longer one unique ruler over Egypt, on the contrary, there could be several kings at the same time, all of them assuming full royal style and claiming full royal power, without challenging similar claims of the others.

On the traditional Egyptian level, however, the title 'King of Upper and Lower Egypt' displayed the *royal* power of Herihor and his successors, which they claimed on account of their role as High Priests of Amun. After the death of Ramesses XI the theocracy of Amun was proclaimed as a new form of government for southern Egypt, being a political realisation – enabled by the death of the last Ramesside king – of theological ideas about a divine lordship of Amun, that had been developed by the priesthood of Amun in Thebes already during the 19th and 20th Dynasties. This enabled the new southern rulers in their capacity of High Priests to represent Amun, the divine sole ruler of Egypt, and to execute his oracular decrees. Though they are no *genuine* kings, they do act in a royal function, thus exercising supreme authority, and the title *King of Upper and Lower Egypt* expresses this royal function. As Jansen-Winkeln convincingly has shown, those High Priests who use royal attributes – Herihor, Pinudjem I, and Menkheperre – count their own regnal years, not in their capacity of High Priests of Amun but by virtue of their royal status.[20] More or less paralleling this development in Upper Egypt, some Lower-Egyptian kings refer in their names and titles to the kingship of Amun, thus manifesting themselves as High-priestly representatives of the divine king Amun.

Though we see a gradual development of declining royal power and increasing influence of Amun and his priesthood, there is by contrast a far-reaching change with the start of the 21st Dynasty. From now on it is no longer the king who rules Egypt, but the god Amun himself; the religious-political tradition is replaced by the theocracy of Amun.

Concerning this rather sudden transition to a new era, the temple of Khonsu in Karnak provides some elucidating information. In the hypostyle hall Herihor is depicted as High Priest of Amun and general, juxtaposed with king Ramesses XI, both of them portrayed on the same scale and performing the same divine offices for the gods.[21] In the peristyle court of the temple, which as usual was decorated after the decoration activities in the hypostyle hall had been finished, Herihor is portrayed as king with the title High Priest of Amun (*Ḥm-nṯr-tpj-n-ꜥImn*) as his prenomen, whereas references to king Ramesses XI are completely absent, suggesting that from the latter's decease Herihor assumed royal dignity, without giving up his High-priestly office. With regard to the decoration of the temple Herihor was succeeded by Pinudjem I, to whom on the pylon of the temple, besides the title High Priest of Amun, elements of royal style were attributed.

During the 19th and 20th Dynasties the highest positions within the priesthood of Amun at Thebes, those of High Priest and Second, Third, and Fourth Prophets, were with some exceptions held by members of a few major Theban priestly families, namely the Bakenkhons family, the family of Tjanefer, and the family of Ramessesnakht.[22] With the advent of the 21st Dynasty this situation changed dramatically. The new southern rulers not only obtained for themselves the post of High Priest of Amun, but they also seem to have been successful in having their sons appointed to other high priestly offices,

---

16 A. Egberts, 'Hard Times: The Chronology of "The Report of Wenamun" Revised', *Zeitschrift für ägyptische Sprache und Altertumskunde* 125 (1998), pp. 100-101.

17 Egberts, 'Chronology of "The Report of Wenamun"', p. 102.

18 A. Leahy, 'The Libyan Period in Egypt: An Essay in Interpretation', *Libyan Studies* 16 (1985), p. 59; R. Ritner, 'Fragmentation and Reintegration in the Third Intermediate Period', in: G.P.F. Broekman *et al.* (eds), *The Libyan Period in Egypt. Historical and Cultural Studies into the 21st -24th Dynasties: Proceedings of a Conference at Leiden University, 25-27 October 2007*, Leiden and Leuven 2009, p. 333.

19 Leahy, *Libyan Studies* pp. 16 and 59.

20 K. Jansen-Winkeln, 'Die thebanischen Gründer der 21. Dynastie', *Göttinger Miszellen* 157 (1997), p. 67.

21 *Cf.* A. Dodson, *Afterglow of Empire. Egypt from the Fall of the New Kingdom to the Saite Renaissance*. Cairo 2012, pp. 21-22.

22 M.R. Bierbrier, *The Late New Kingdom in Egypt (c.1300-664 B.C.) A Genealogical and Chronological Investigation*, Warminster 1975, pp. 2-13.

though due to a scarcity of information the succession to the posts of Second, Third, and Fourth Prophets of Amun during the first half of the 21st Dynasty is unclear. In this period the only known occupants of these posts are Herihor's son the Third Prophet of Amun and Overseer of the cattle of $P_3\ r^c$ Ankhefenamun, and the second prophet of Amun Heqanefer, a brother of Pinudjem I.[23]

It may be clear that the members of the Theban priesthood of Amun, who during the 18th to 20th Dynasties had obtained immense political and economic power, were displeased with their new overlords monopolizing the most important and lucrative Theban offices, and this might have caused the problems that are referred to by the High Priest Menkheperre (A), son of king Pinudjem I, in the so-called Banishment Stela,[24] recording the victorious entry of Menkheperre in Thebes, the god Amun installing him in his father's position of High Priest of Amun and issuing an oracular decree regarding the return of a number of exiles from the oases.[25]

From this text it is clear that Menkheperre was forced to make concessions to the Thebans. and it may be assumed that as a result of these concessions the posts of Second, Third, and Fourth Prophets of Amun henceforth were held by members of other Theban families, whom the High Priests of Amun endeavoured to link with their own family by means of marriage alliances.[26] Thus, the Fourth Prophet of Amun Tjanefer (A), son of the Fourth Prophet of Amun Nespaherenmut, married Gautseshen A, daughter of the High Priest of Amun Menkheperre A.

From fragment 3A of the Karnak Priestly Annals it appears that in Year 40, presumably of Menkheperre, this Tjanefer conducted an inspection of Theban temples.[27] The same Tjanefer A is mentioned in an oracle text inscribed on the tenth pylon in Karnak, concerning the confirmation of the proprietary rights of Henttawy, widow of Nesubanebdjed (Smendes II), and her daughter Istemkheb.[28] The original text almost completely get lost, and we only have some copies. The earliest copy, made by Champollion, only contains the first ten lines of the oracle text. In this part of the text, in which the years 5, 6 and 8 of an unnamed king are mentioned, Tjanefer, apparently promoted to Third Prophet of Amun, acts together with the High Priest of Amun Pinudjem (II).[29] Further down in the badly mutilated oracle text, copied by Maspero, Tjanefer is called Second Prophet of Amun.[30] Those years 5, 6 and 8 might refer to king Amenemope as well as to king Siamun,[31] and are in either case within the pontificate of Pinudjem II, as he held the office of High Priest of Amun from shortly after the start of Amenemope's reign until year 10 of Siamun.[32]

In another oracle, inscribed near the tenth pylon, clearing the God's Father of Amun Thutmose, son of Suawyamun, of several charges of fraud, the Third Prophet of Amun Tjanefer A is represented together with a Fourth Prophet of Amun, whose name is illegible.[33] In this oracle the years 2, 3 and 5 of an unnamed king are mentioned, and because also in this oracle Pinudjem II appears, the years mentioned may refer either to Amenemope or to Osochor or to Siamun.

Tjanefer's involvement in these oracles reflects the influence of the priests of Amun on social and political affairs in the Thebaid. The great oracle processes of Amun usually took place in the southern courts of the temple of Amun at Karnak, and the High Priest together with the other Priests of Amun involved in the oracle procedure actually disclosed the oracular decisions.

No wonder that the members of the priesthood of Amun strove to pass their influential priestly offices on to their descendants, and indeed, transition of priestly

---

23   With respect to Ankhefenamun see *The Epigraphic Survey, The Temple of Khonsu – Volume I, Scenes of King Herihor in the Court*, Oriental Institute Publications 100, Chicago 1979, p. 11, pl. 26. Note that Ankhefenamun's title '*Overseer of the cattle of $P_3\ r^c$*' may be an abbreviation of *Superintendent of the cattle of the roof-temple of Re in the temple of Amun*, a title frequently found in combination with the title Third Prophet of Amun. The legend to the picture of Ankhefenamun in the temple of Amun was wrongly read *Pareamunenamun* by H. Gauthier, *Le Livre des rois d'Égypte, Volume III*, Cairo 1915, p. 238. This faulty rendering of the name was copied by H. Kees, K.A. Kitchen and A. Dodson. As to Heqanefer see K. Jansen-Winkeln, *Inschriften der Spätzeit, Teil I: Die 21. Dynastie*, Wiesbaden 2007, p. 17 [3.22].

24   Louvre inv. no. C. 256, cf. e.g. H. Sternberg-el Hotabi, 'Die Stele der Verbannten', in: *Texte aus der Umwelt des Alten Testaments* II/1, Gütersloh 1986, pp. 112-116.

25   Louvre inv. no. C. 256. See Jansen-Winkeln, *Inschriften I*, pp. 72-74 [6.1].

26   K.A. Kitchen, *The Third Intermediate Period in Egypt (1100-650 BC)³*, Warminster 1995, p. 276.

27   Jansen-Winkeln, *Inschriften I*, pp. 74-75 [6. 3].

28   A. Gardiner, 'The Gods of Thebes as Guarantors of Personal Property', *Journal of Egyptian Archaeology* 48 (1962), pp. 57-69.

29   J.-F. Champollion, *Notices descriptives*, Part 2, Reprogr., Genève 1972-1973, pp. 178-179.

30   G. Maspero, 'Notes sur quelques points de Grammaire et d'Histoire', *Zeitschrift für ägyptische Sprache und Altertumskunde* 21 (1883), pp. 73-74; G. Maspero, 'Les Momies royales de Déir el Bahari', *Mémoires publiés par les membres de la mission archéologique française au Caire* 1, Cairo 1889, pp. 704-706. It should be noticed that the title Second Prophet of Amun, assigned to Tjanefer, may be erroneous, in view of the fact that he was buried as Third Prophet.

31   It is improbable that these years refer to king Osochor, as he reigned only six years, and attribution of years 5 and 6 to Osochor would imply that year 8 should be attributed to Siamun, resulting in an improbably long duration of the oracle proceedings (more than ten years).

32   From a graffito at the entrance of the Royal Cache (TT 320) it is clear that Pinudjem II was buried in year 10 of Siamun. Jansen-Winkeln, *Inschriften I*, pp. 141 [9. 33].

33   J.-M. Kruchten, *Le grand texte oraculaire de Djéhoutymose*, Brussels 1986, pp. 294-324; Jansen-Winkeln, *Inschriften I*, pp. 170-177 [11. 8].

titles from father to son is more than once shown in the Karnak Priestly Annals, for instance on a block found in the Karnak storehouse Sheik Labib.[34] On this block three consecutive texts are shown. The first one records the introduction of one Nesamun into the temple of Amun in Karnak, the so-called *Great and Venerable Chapel of Amun*, during the reign of Siamun, his regnal year being illegible. The second text, dated to regnal year eleven of Psusennes II, mentions the introduction of Nesamun's son Nesankhefenmaat. The third text, finally, dated to the third year of Osorkon I, refers to the introduction of Hor, son of Nesankhefenmaat and grandson of Nesamun. A similar development is found with respect to the family of Tjanefer A, whom his sons Pinudjem A and Menkheperre B succeeded as Fourth and Third Prophet of Amun respectively. We derive this knowledge from their burial assemblages, found together with the grave goods of their parents Tjanefer A and Gautseshen A in the second room of the *Bab el-Gasus*.

2.3 The *Bab el-Gasus* cache

This underground tomb in the courtyard of Hatshepsut's mortuary temple has been used as a cache for the burials of 153 priests and chantresses of Amun, all of whom date to the 21st Dynasty. Concerning the history of the cache no unanimity exists. Formerly it has been claimed that the tomb was originally built in the 19th Dynasty and that it was extended in the 21st Dynasty for the family of Menkheperre A.[35] Niwiński opines that "it would seem that the tomb had been hewn in the 21st Dynasty, under the pontificate of HP Psusennes, and was intended as a burial place for the priests of Amun from the beginning".[36] According to Saphinaz-Amal Naguib the *Bab el-Gasus* was used as a catacomb for the Amun priesthood already from the pontificate of Menkheperre.[37] And finally David Aston, in his comprehensive work *Burial Assemblages of Dynasty 21-25*, argues: As none of the grave goods within the cache can be dated later than the pontificate of Psusennes 'III', it is reasonable to assume that this cache was created during the pontificate of that High Priest, an assumption that fits well with Niwiński's suggestion that the cache is no earlier than Year 1 of Psusennes II. The presence of the family group Tjanefer A, Pinedjem A, Gautseshen A/i and Menkheperre B at the very end of the tomb suggests that it was this family who first reused this tomb, and that shortly afterwards it was chosen as a suitable location for a cache.[38]

From the position of the coffins at the time of the discovery of the intact tomb, something may be concluded concerning its history. It appears that the second room, at the very end of the tomb, initially served as the burial chamber of the Tjanefer A family. Four, and perhaps even five, out of the nine coffin ensembles in this room belonged to this family. Apart from Tjanefer A and his wife and sons, also the coffins of the Fourth Prophet of Amun Nesamun v were found in this chamber, suggesting that he belongs to the same family, which seems to be corroborated by the partly gilding of his coffins, characteristic of the coffins of descendants of Menkheperre A. The four remaining burials in this room belong to a child called Tjanefer, an anonymous young child, an anonymus w^cb-priest of Amun, and a chantress of Amun named Djedmutesankh.

Aston is probably right in arguing that the *Bab el-Gasus*, shortly after the second room was put into use for the reinterment of the Tjanefer family, was destined as location for a cache. It is obvious that the rear parts of the tomb would be filled first of all, and it appears that the first room, adjacent to the second room, contained the burials of five members of the High-Priestly family, namely Menkheperre A's sons Hor and Ankhefenmut and his granddaughter Harweben, and the chantress of Amun Tawedjatre, who might be daughter of the High Priest of Amun Masaharta and niece of Menkheperre A. The four remaining coffins in this room belonged to chantresses of Amun. One of them, named Gautseshen (B), might be a daughter of Menkheperre B and great-granddaughter of Menkheperre A. At the end of the main corridor, close to the entrance of the first room, the coffin of Maatkare daughter of Pinudjem II was found, and in the lateral corridor, near its entrance, the coffin of another daughter of Menkheperre A, named Meret-Amun, was placed.

Thus, it appears that at first the coffins of the High Priests family were put in safety, at the very end of the tomb. Amongst the owners of these coffins were almost all leading members – with the exception of the High Priests themselves – of the Amun priesthood, the Second (?), Third and Fourth Prophets. Only the coffin of the Fourth Prophet of Amun Nespaherentahat, who had usurped this coffin from an individual named Padiamun, was found rather close to the entrance of the main corridor, whereas no burial ensemble of Tjanefer A's father, the Fourth, later Third, Prophet of Amun Nespaherenmut, was found.

---

34 Block Sheik Labib 94 CL 2149, numbered 142b. See F. Payraudeau, 'De nouvelles annales sacerdotales de Siamon, Psousennès II et Osorkon Ier', *Bulletin de l'Institut Français d'Archéologie Orientale* 108 (2008), pp. 293-308.
35 A. Niwiński, 'The Bab el-Gasus Tomb and the Royal Cashe in Deir el-Bahri', *Journal of Egyptian Archaeology* 70 (1984), pp. 74-75, with references.
36 Niwiński, *21st Dynasty Coffins*, p. 26.
37 S.-A. Naguib, *Le Clergé Féminin d'Amon Thébain à la 21e Dynastie*, Leuven 1990, p. 118.

38 D.A. Aston, *Burial Assemblages of Dynasty 21-25. Chronology – Typology – Development*, Vienna 2009, p. 198.

It would seem that the other coffin ensembles in the *Bab el-Gasus*, some twenty of which had been usurped from their original owners, had been placed quite arbitrarily along the corridors, suggesting that they were brought in without observance of any specific order, the lateral corridor and the rear part of the main corridor being filled first, and next the foremost part of the main corridor. Niwiński pointed out, that "in spite of the fact that there was much room far inside the tomb, the coffins near the entrance were crowded. This would seem to imply that the last coffins had been hastily put into the cache".[39] Quite a lot of the coffinensembles contained leather mummy braces and/or pendelogues, showing the name of the reigning king or of the High Priest who was in office at the time of the burial. As the name of the High Priest Psusennes III is the latest one mentioned on these braces and pendelogues, it may be assumed – in accordance with Aston – that the coffins were placed during his pontificate.[40]

2.4 Other Collective Cache Burials

The *Bab el-Gasus* was not the only collective tomb from the 21st Dynasty, and according to Dodson, collective burials seem to have been the norm in Thebes during this period.[41]

We have here another phenomenon characteristic of the 21st Dynasty. From the outset of the Pharaonic era each deceased king as well as each deceased individual who could afford it, was buried in his own tomb, sometimes together with his wife or other members of his family, and provided with a more or less extensive burial ensemble, including a tomb chapel, statuary and decorated coffin(s). After the tomb robberies during the second half of the 20th Dynasty, the Egyptian elite abandoned family tombs with decorated aboveground chapels, opting instead for hidden collective cache burials.

One of these collective tombs is the so-called Royal Cache, usually referred to as Theban Tomb (TT) 320, located next to Deir el-Bahari in the Theban necropolis. The entrance of the tomb was found by members of the local Abd el-Rasul family in 1871, and served subsequently as a store of precious articles that were sold on the antiquities market. This caused the local authorities to investigate and locate the source of these items. The track led to the Abd el-Rasul family, and after many harsh examinations and a quarrel within the Abd el-Rasul family, the eldest brother Mohammed showed in July 1881 the entrance of the tomb to Emil Brugsch, the assistant of the director-general of excavations and of the antiquities of Egypt, George Maspero.

The tomb is thought to have initially been used as the family tomb of Pinudjem II, his two wives Istemkheb D and Nesikhonsu A, and his daughter Nesitanebashru. According to Aston, "this tomb was begun in the 18th Dynasty and was subsequently enlarged by Pinedjem II to serve as a family tomb for his own family".[42] From graffiti near the bottom of the shaft it appears that the burial of Pinudjem II's wife Nesikhonsu in the tomb took placed in year 5, and Pinudjem's own burial in year 10, both years apparently referring to king Siamun. Subsequently the Royal Cache served as the final burial place for the 21st Dynasty High Priests of Amun Pinudjem I and his son Masaharta, whereas the burial places of the High Priests Menkheperre A and his son Smendes II are unknown, nor do we have anything that might have belonged to their burial ensembles, suggesting that these still survive intact.[43]

From the braces and bandages on the mummy of Djedptahiufankh A, probably son-in-law of Pinudjem II, it appears that he was interred in the Royal Cache not before Shoshenq I's tenth regnal year, and it is not clear whether all reinterments of royal mummies in the cache took place in the 21st Dynasty, or some of them were placed in the tomb after Djedptahiufankh.

Anyway, we may assume that throughout the Dynasty the Theban priesthood was involved in the ongoing program of restoration and reinterment of the New Kingdom royal mummies buried in their tombs in the Kings' Valley, which apparently was a major concern of the High Priests of Amun. Evidence of renewal of the royal burials was found on dockets on their coffins and newly manufactured mummy-linen, referring to the High Priests Pinudjem I, Menkheperre A and Pinudjem II, as well as to king Siamun. It appears that many of the coffins found in the Royal Cache, including those of Pinudjem I and his family, have had most of their gilding or gilded elements removed, whereas in several cases religious texts and divine images were left more or less intact.[44] As Karl Jansen-Winkeln already in 1995 pointed out, the fact that the gilding and gilded elements were *painstakingly* removed from the royal coffins, suggests that this was not done by thieves but by the priests and officials who were in charge of the reburial. In this connection Jansen-Winkeln points to the fact that in the 21st Dynasty Amun is the divine king of Egypt, who is entitled to dispose of the economically indispensable treasures on hand in the tombs of the ancient kings, who no longer were considered gods.[45]

---

39 Niwiński, *21st Dynasty Coffins*, p. 26.
40 *Cf.* Niwiński, *21st Dynasty Coffins*, p. 26.
41 Dodson, *Afterglow of Empire*, p. 62.

42 Aston, *Burial Assemblages*, p. 220.
43 See in this connection Dodson, *Afterglow of Empire*, p. 65.
44 Dodson, *Afterglow of Empire*, p. 62.
45 K. Jansen-Winkeln, 'Die Plünderung der Köningsgräber des Neues Reiches', *Zeitschrift für ägyptische Sprache und Altertumskunde* 122 (1995), pp. 62-78.

2.5 The End of the 21st Dynasty

Not only in Thebes but as well in Lower Egypt collective tombs were the vogue. On the royal necropolis in Tanis, inside the enclosure wall of the great temple of Amun, two royal tombs adjacent to each other were found in 1939 by the French Egyptologist Pierre Montet. One of these tombs, Royal Necropolis of Tanis (NRT) tomb I, in which the burials of the 22nd Dynasty king Osorkon II, his father Takeloth II, and his prematurely deceased son prince Hornakht were found, is broadly thought to initially have been the tomb of the founder of the 21st Dynasty Smendes I.

The adjacent tomb, NRT III, which at its discovery appeared to be undisturbed, comprised the burial-chambers of king Psusennes I and his spouse queen Mutnedjmet, her burial-chamber, however, being usurped by Psusennes' successor Amenemope.[46] In the third burial-room accessible from the vestibule of the tomb, the empty sarcophagus of the king's son Ankhefenmut C was found, and a fourth chamber, only accessible from above after removing some roofing blocks, comprised the undisturbed burial ensemble of the high dignitary Wendejebaendjed, superintendent of the courtiers of Psusennes I. In the vestibule of the tomb three secondary burials were found, one of them being the enigmatic king Shoshenq (II) Heqakheperre, apparently belonging to the 22nd Dynasty. The identity of the individuals flanking Shoshenq's silver coffin is difficult to be established, since their burials were relatively poor, with their mummies completely decayed, though it appears from the uraeii that had been affixed to the coffins, that these burials are of royal persons. The presence in the vestibule of Psusennes' tomb of two *shabti* groups, bearing the names Siamun and Psusennes, strongly suggests that the anonymous burials in the vestibule of NRT III are to be attributed to the kings Siamun and Psusennes II respectively, who obviously were reinterred in this tomb.[47] Psusennes II, mentioned by Manetho as the last king of the 21st Dynasty, is to be identified with king Tytkheperre Setepenre (Hor-)Pasebakhaenniut Meryamun (*Tjt-ḫpr-Rꜥ Stp-n-Rꜥ (Ḥr-)Pꜣ-sbꜣ-ḫꜥ-n-njwt Mry-ʾImn*), known from the monumental evidence.[48] Whereas this identification is undisputed, it is a question whether he is identical with the Theban High Priest of Amun of the same name, as some contemporary sources seem to be contradictory in this respect. The bandage epigraph on the mummy of the chantress of Amun Tentpenherunefer from the *Bab el-Gasus*, mentioning The High Priest of Amun Psusennes (III), also mentions a year date which Daressy read as 'Year 4' and later as 'Year 5'. If this is correct, it would indicate that Psusennes III must be a separate individual to Psusennes II.[49] On the other hand a hieratic graffito in the temple of Seti I in Abydos would, according to Jansen-Winkeln, suggest that Psusennes II is identical with Pinudjem II's son Psusennes III, and that "he was king and at the same time HP (High Priest) in Thebes; he had clearly not resigned this office".[50]

In case Psusennes III was not identical with king Psusennes II, he would have succeeded his father Pinudjem II as High Priest of Amun in year 10 of Siamun and would probably have died early in the reign of Shoshenq I, to be succeeded by the latter's son Iuput A. If, on the other hand, Psusennes II and Psusennes III were one and the same individual (Psusennes II/III) he would have been High Priest from year 10 of Siamun until the latter's death, probably in his nineteenth regnal year, and from then on in the twofold capacity of king and High Priest of Amun till his death, probably in his own fourteenth regnal year.

Though the transition from the 21st to the 22nd Dynasty passed smoothly, Shoshenq I, the founder of the new Dynasty, aimed from the outset of his reign at curbing the power of the Theban Amun clergy. "From then on members of the royal family were appointed to the leading posts, headed by the king's son Iuput as High Priest of Amun, Army Commander and Governor of Upper Egypt".[51]

After in the final years of Psusennes II the last coffins, including the Leiden inner and outer coffins F 93/10.2a-b of the chantress of Amun Nesytanebtawy, were brought inside the *Bab el-Gasus* cache, the entrance of the main corridor was bricked up and next the shaft was filled up with a mixture of stones, sand and clay. Soon afterwards anything that might point to the presence of the subterranean tomb had disappeared under the sands of the desert without leaving any traces. Ever since the *Bab el-Gasus* remained undisturbed until it was discovered by the director of the Département des Antiquitées Égyptiennes Eugène Grébaut and his assistant Georges Daressy on 4 February 1891 (see chapter 3).

---

46 P. Montet, *La nécropole royale de Tanis II: Les constructions et le tombeau de Psousennes à Tanis*, Paris 1951.
47 Aston, *Burial Assemblages*, p. 51; J. Yoyotte, 'Tanis', in: J.-L. de Cénival and J. Yoyotte (eds), *Tanis, L'or des Pharaons*, Paris 1987, p. 48.
48 Cf. Jansen-Winkeln, in: *Ancient Egyptian Chronology*, pp. 220-221.
49 Aston, *Burial Assemblages*, pp. 166-167.
50 Jansen-Winkeln, in *Ancient Egyptian Chronology*, p. 223. See also in this connection A. Dodson, 'The Transition between the 21st and 22nd Dynasties Revisited', in: G.P.F. Broekman et al. (eds), *The Libyan Period in Egypt*, Leiden 2009, pp. 104-108; Dodson, *Afterglow of Empire*, pp. 78-79.
51 Van Walsem, *Djedmonthuiufankh*, p. 362.

Chapter 3

The Tomb of the Priests of Amun at Thebes: The History of the Find

Rogério Sousa

3.1 Introduction

Bab el-Gasus, also known as the Tomb of the Priests of Amun, is located outside the north-eastern corner of the Hatshepsut temple-precinct. This site, the largest undisturbed tomb ever found in Egypt, was discovered in 1891, just ten years after the 'Royal Cache' (1881). Given this association, the site came to be known in Egyptology literature by several designations, such as '*Deuxieme Trouvaille de Deir el-Bahari*' or even the 'Cache of the Priests'. These names had been translated by the local workmen into the Arabic dialect used in Gurnah and may have resulted in the designation of the tomb as Bab el-Gaswasa, meaning the 'Gate of the Priests', later wrongly interpreted by archaeologists as *Bab el-Gasus* or *Bab el-Gusus*, both corrupted versions of the original expression.[52] For the sake of commodity we will keep using in this text the expression *Bab el-Gasus*, the commonly accepted designation of the tomb.

The site was first spotted by Mohammed Ahmed Abd el-Rassul.[53] In January 1891 Eugène Grébaut was the head of the Egyptian Antiquities Service, replacing Gaston Maspero, who had returned to France shortly before, in 1886. At that time, when Grébaut was involved in the clearance of the uppermost part of the Hatshepsut temple in Deir el-Bahari, Rassul revealed to him his suspicions about the existence of a previously unnoticed tomb in the area next to the first courtyard of Hatshepsut's temple.[54]

Following his advice Grébaut started to clear the area and it soon became evident that Rassul's instinct had proved correct. The reason that the tomb was not discovered earlier lies in its efficient blocking system. The entrance to the tomb had been sealed with a multi-layered system of large stones protruding from the surface and concealing an asymmetrically arranged pavement of limestone slabs. Under these slabs a thick layer of mud bricks covered yet another stone pavement sealing the top of the shaft, which was

---

52 We owe this information to our colleague, Dr. Eltayed Abbas, who inquired the inhabitants of the village concerning the local toponymy of the site. We arrived to the same conclusion during our field season in 2009.
53 This famous villager from Gurnah also revealed the existence of the so-called 'Royal Cache' in 1881 (TT 320). In G. Daressy, 'Les sépultures des prêtres d'Ammon à Deir el-Bahari', *Annales du Service des Antiquités de l'Égypte* 1 (1900), p. 142.
54 Daressy, *Annales du Service des Antiquités de l'Égypte* 1, p. 142.

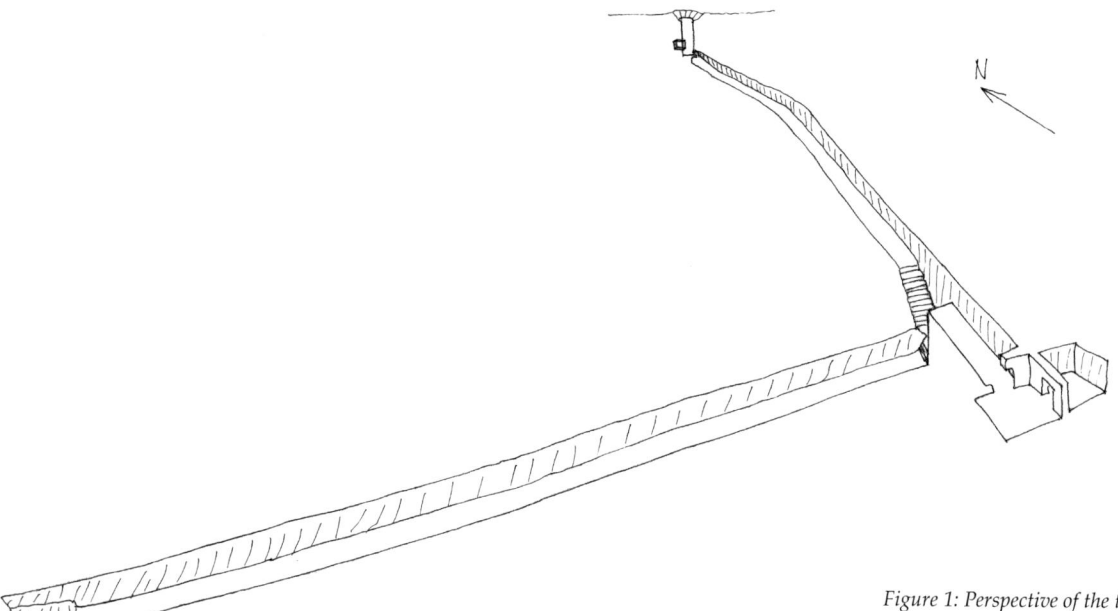

Figure 1: Perspective of the tomb. Drawing by Rogério Sousa.

filled with rock debris to a depth of about eight meters. At this level, a small side-chamber was found, carved into the northern wall. The entrance to this room was blocked with tree branches, chunks of stone and pieces of broken coffins.[55]

Below this chamber, a false pavement consisting of reed mats and tree trunks concealed the way down to the bottom of the shaft, located eleven meters below the surface and filled with large stones and sand. Here, the excavators found a doorway in the southern wall sealed with mud bricks.[56]

At this stage, Grébaut called his younger colleague Georges Daressy, who was then working at the Luxor Temple, to assist him in exploring the tomb. The involvement of Georges Daressy, a diligent and meticulous scholar, in this process was quite providential since his records, later published in the *Annales du Service des Antiquités d'Égypte*,[57] remained the only available source for the original composition of the find.

3.2 The Opening of the Tomb

The impressions recorded by Daressy provide a vivid account of his exploration of the tomb. The doorway was opened on 4 February 1891. It revealed a long undecorated corridor hewn out of the rock, 1.70 to 1.90 meters wide, and of a similar height (Fig. 1). It was immediately clear that this was a collective burial ground holding a vast number of individuals. The corridor was filled with scores of anthropoid coffins, most heading south. When Daressy entered the tomb, the heat was stifling but – he states – "it did not smell bad".[58] The style of decoration on the coffins suggested that this tomb dated from the end of the 21st Dynasty (1069-945 BCE). The tomb had provided excellent conditions for the preservation of the burial sets for almost 3000 years and the objects were

---

55 Daressy, *Annales du Service des Antiquités de l'Égypte* 1, p. 142.
56 Daressy, *Annales du Service des Antiquités de l'Égypte* 1, p. 142. We have seen (chapter 2) that the 21st Dynasty was a period that witnessed frequent tomb robberies and the Priests of Amun took great – and indeed successful – measures to save their burials from disturbances.
57 Daressy, *Annales du Service des Antiquités de l'Égypte* 1, pp. 141-148.
58 Daressy, *Annales du Service des Antiquités de l'Égypte* 1, p. 142.

Figure 2: View of the main corridor with the burial chambers on the background. Photograph by the Egyptian expedition, Metropolitan Museum of Art, New York, 1924. Copyright: Metropolitan Museum of Art.

in perfect condition.⁵⁹ Each mummy was buried within a coffin set normally composed of an outer coffin which held within an inner coffin and a mummycover, besides a variable number of other small funerary artefacts. The coffin sets have been arranged against the walls, usually in pairs, with one coffin set over the other, leaving a space in between for easy access to the innermost areas of the tomb. However, next to the entrance, barriers were formed by putting three sets of coffins side by side and three others on top of them.⁶⁰ Four barriers of this kind were created in this way shortly before the definitive sealing of the tomb, which suggests that the coffins themselves were used as part of the tomb's blocking system. Between the coffin sets, in no apparent order, there were wooden Osiris statues, vessels and canopic jars. The floor was littered with the remains of floral garlands and fruit, broken *shabtis* and fragments of coffins. *Shabti*-boxes with one or two compartments were located randomly in the galleries, sometimes far from the original burial assemblage. Some collections of *shabtis* were found in baskets, while others had simply been left on the floor.⁶¹

The main corridor was 93 meters long and led south, where two adjoining square chambers of roughly equal size were found. Along this gallery, seven niches were cut into the east wall for lamps. These niches were carved at 1.50 m intervals from the floor and still presented vestiges of white wax which had melted and run down the wall.

At a short distance from the end chambers (76.2 meters from the entrance) Daressy found a second, nearly perpendicular passage. It was carved at a lower level, two meters below the floor of the main gallery and was nearly 52.4 meters long and 1.50 meters wide. Four niches were cut into the north wall of this gallery for lamps. This transversal gallery was left unfinished but it is possible that a burial chamber might have been planned for this corridor.⁶²

However, reaching the transversal gallery was not exempt from dangers. On approaching the southern funerary chambers, Daressy found a stairway which abruptly narrowed to half its width, creating a deep shaft on the right-hand side (Fig. 2). Next to the rear wall the stairway veers west leaving a single square slab at the turning point.

It was clear that this unusual stairway was designed to elude potential intruders and keep the burial chambers out of sight, thus forming a sophisticated defensive system.⁶³ Because of that, the large number of burials found in the two funerary chambers necessarily had to be moved up using ladders and ropes.

Despite the care involved in increasing the security of the tomb, Daressy noticed intriguing clues suggesting that a methodical plunder of the burials took place even before its definitive sealing. While removing the coffin sets from the tomb, Daressy and his team opened the burial assemblages and pulled up separately the outer coffins and the inner coffins. While doing so he remarked that the exterior coffins of the double sets were often found unlocked, whereas the inner coffins remained sealed. Such pattern resulted from the method used by the Egyptian priests themselves: they had opened up the burial sets and lowered the inner and outer coffins down separately. Perhaps deliberately, when they placed the burial sets in their final location in the tomb the ancient undertakers

---

59 Daressy, *Annales du Service des Antiquités de l'Égypte* 1, p. 145. However, when the ancient sealed site was opened, the fresh air caused the gesso covering of many of the coffins to crack, a phenomenon caused by sudden atmospheric changes.
60 Daressy, *Annales du Service des Antiquités de l'Égypte* 1, p. 143.
61 Sometimes several types of *shabtis* were found in the same container, but in other cases it was not possible to match the name on the objects to their original burial assemblage. See Daressy, *Annales du Service des Antiquités de l'Égypte* 8, p. 12.
62 Niwiński, *Journal of Egyptian Archaeology* 70, p. 74.
63 Daressy, *Annales du Service des Antiquités de l'Égypte* 1, p. 142.

Figure 3: Coffin set of Hory (A.143), at the Egyptian Museum in Cairo (JE 29619). Photo: Rogério Sousa.

Figure 4: Outer coffin of Hory (detail of the head-board and upper section). Photo: Rogério Sousa.

Figure 5: Third coffin of Hory (detail of the head-board and upper section). Photo: Rogério Sousa.

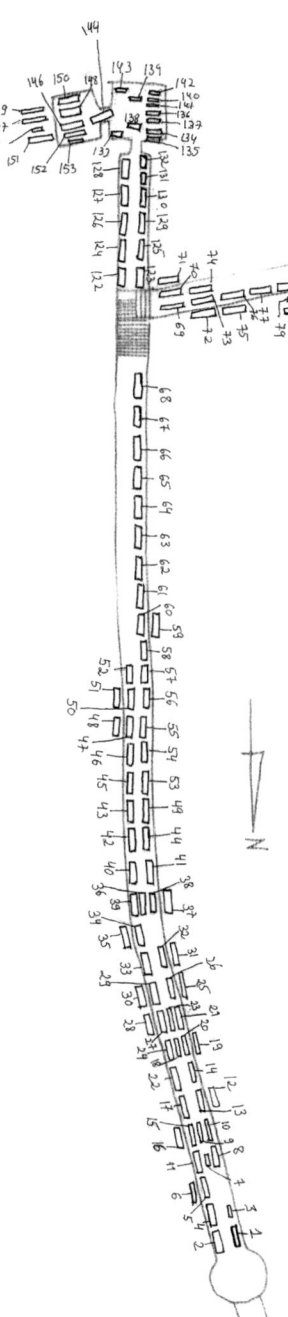

Figure 6: Plan of the tomb with the original position of the burial sets. Drawing by the author after Niwiński, 21st Dynasty Coffins from Thebes, table 1. The present drawing includes the original burial chamber located in the shaft and the reviewed position of the burials, according to the notes published by Daressy (Daressy, Annales du Service des Antiquités de l'Égypte 1, pp. 147-148).

did not lock them.[64] The fact is that some of the coffin sets reveal intriguing traces of plunder, after their storage in the tomb (Fig. 3).

The outer coffin of Hory, the son of the High Priest Menkheperre and owner of one of the finest burial assemblages of the tomb, was left undisturbed, but the inner coffins were plundered and their faces and hands were ripped off to remove the gold (Figs 4-5).[65]

Further evidence of this type of plunder is found in the most splendid coffins buried in the tomb,[66] suggesting that the looting of *Bab el-Gasus*, was carried out by the personnel that managed the site. In fact, the selective looting could only have been possible by well-informed individuals that had plain access to the most important areas of the tomb (compare p. 18).

It is interesting to note that Daressy still found fragments of beards and hands in a box. These objects were left behind probably because the amount of gold involved in the decoration of the faces was superior. It is thus possible that the faces have been first taken out of the tomb and that the remaining objects were kept in a safe deposit waiting to be removed. The beards, in particular, were almost useless in terms of recycling the gilded foil and for that reason they were reaped off the faces to provide a better handling of the objects while moving them outside, probably hidden under the clothes.

The fact is that, when the tomb was sealed, with its 153 coffin sets buried inside its galleries, it was still well below its storage capacity, which could have easily held at least more 70 coffin sets, if not more (Fig. 6).

All these clues suggest that the sealing of the tomb was unexpected and that it remained open during a relatively short period of time. The closure of the tomb was probably anticipated to prevent the occurrence of further damage to the main burials kept in the burial chambers. However, further evidence suggests that a 'last visit' to the burial chambers took place shortly before the final closure of the tomb. Daressy points out in his report that in the stairway moving down to the transversal gallery, a ladder had been improvised by propping a coffin lid against the wall to provide access to the funerary chambers. He found the lid still in position, with the foot-board, hands and face scratched from having served as a stairway.[67] This piece of evidence once again suggests that not only the sealing of the tomb was unexpected as the personnel involved in the storage of the coffins inside the tomb somehow 'mapped' the potential resources provided by the burials and carried out a selective plunder.

---

64   G. Daressy, 'Contribution à l'étude de la XXI Dynastie Égyptienne', *Révue Archaeologique*, 3 (1896), p. 73.

65   Unlike most of the coffins sets dating from this period, the burial assemblage of Hory (A.143) included three coffins. The information provided by Daressy is surprisingly scarce about this coffin set and its equipment. See Daressy, *Annales du Service des Antiquités de l'Égypte* 8, pp. 36-37.

66   Daressy, *Annales du Service des Antiquités de l'Égypte* 1, p. 143. These coffins used gilded foil with symbolic purposes, especially in the decoration of the face and hands, where it suggested the association of the deceased with the immortal light of the sun god.

67   Daressy, *Annales du Service des Antiquités de l'Égypte* 1, p. 142.

Figure 7: The removal of the coffins from Bab el-Gasus. Illustration by Émile Bayard published on the cover of the nº 2510 of L´Illustration on 4 April 1891 (with thanks to Dik van Bommel). Eugène Grébaut is depicted below the tent leaning against the balustrade. Georges Daressy is recording the objects.

The definitive proof of this methodical activity was eventually given by the mummies themselves. When, later on, Daressy and his assistants examined the mummies, it became obvious that a selective looting had affected the most important mummies[68] before the final sealing of the tomb.

3.3 The Removal of the Coffins and Burial Equipment from the Tomb

On 5 February 1891 the archaeologists started to clear the tomb by removing the funerary goods outside. This process was performed in two steps. Inside the galleries, Daressy numbered the coffin sets with labels glued to the headboard (the numbers form

---

68   A.130, A.132 and A.143.

LES NOUVELLES DÉCOUVERTES DE MOMIES, DANS LA HAUTE-ÉGYPTE. — Transport des sarcophages de Deir-el-Bahari au Nil.
Dessin d'après nature de M. Émile Bayard.

Figure 8: Procession of bearers carrying the coffins towards the steamer. Illustration by Émille Bayard published on the n° 2510 of L'Illustration on 4 April 1891 (with thanks to Dik van Bommel).

the later A-list[69]) according to the position they occupied in the tomb, beginning with the ones closest to the entrance.

Outside, a gang of workmen lifted the finds up from the shaft, under the supervision of Eugène Grébaut and Urbain Bouriant, the Director of the *Institut Français d'Archaeologie Oriental* (Fig. 7). When receiving the objects, Bouriant assigned a serial number to each one (the later B-list[70]). The clearance of the tomb took only nine days (from 5 to 13 February 1891).

In a third step, the objects were loaded onto a Giza Museum steamer anchored on the banks of the Nile. Twice a day, a procession of bearers carried the finds across the flood plain, to be loaded onto the steamer. Émile Bayard, a French traveller visiting the site – and the only outsider allowed to enter the tomb[71] – witnessed the impressive cortege of 200 men carrying 30 lavishly decorated coffins (Fig. 8).

Clad in their traditional garments or naked, these men sang to accompany their steps as they journeyed all the way down to the Nile,[72] forming – in his words – an "unforgettable vision."[73] With part of the objects kept in the steamer and the other remaining in the tomb, Grébaut had to assure the protection of both. He thus employed armed guards as well as the crew of the steamer to assure the safety of the find. Daressy himself took

---

69 Daressy, *Annales du Service des Antiquités de l'Égypte* 8, p. 3.
70 Daressy, *Annales du Service des Antiquités de l'Égypte* 8, p. 3.
71 Daressy, *Annales du Service des Antiquités de l'Égypte* 1, p. 143.
72 E. Bayard, 'Les découvertes de Louqsor', *L'Illustration* 49 (1891), p. 304.
73 Bayard, *L'Illustration* 49, p. 304.

personal care of the security of the tomb and, during this period, he slept in a tent near the entrance to the shaft.[74]

The final list of objects cleared from the tomb and brought on board included:

- 254 coffins (153 coffin sets, 101 of which included two coffins whilst 52 had single coffins)[75]
- 110 *shabti*-boxes
- 77 wooden statuettes of Osiris. Most of them were hollow and contained a papyrus scroll
- 8 wooden stelae
- 2 large wooden statuettes of Isis and Nephthys
- 16 canopic jars
- 1 mat
- 10 baskets of reeds
- 5 round baskets
- 2 fans
- 5 pairs of sandals
- 11 baskets with food (meat, fruits, etc.)
- 6 baskets with floral garlands
- 5 large vases
- 5 pots
- 1 box with wooden hands and divine beards ripped from the coffins

With its precious cargo finally secure on board, the vessel could then set off downriver to Cairo, arriving at the Giza Museum in the beginning of May. Here, the material was registered in the *Journal d'Entrée*, creating a third serial list of numbers (i.e. the JE-numbers).[76]

3.4 Unwrapping of the *Bab el-Gasus* Mummies

The mummies brought from *Bab el-Gasus* were unwrapped in two stages. Most of the mummies were unwrapped between 1891 and 1892,[77] in the premises of the Giza Museum, but this process would only be completed in the Egyptian Museum in Cairo, from 1903 on. During this period, the methods used in the examination of the mummies evolved considerably and the records published by Daressy and his assistants witness to this transformation, beginning with the unwrapping process focused on the inventory of objects found within each mummy. By the turn of the 20th century, this process involved a considerable greater attention to the study of the medical aspects involving the corpses.

3.4.1 The Early Years 1891-1892: Unwrappings at the Giza Museum

Almost immediately after the arrival of the find, Daniel M. Fouquet – a French physician who had first examined the TT 320 royal mummies – began to unwrap the human remains, under Daressy's supervision.[78]

Taking place in the magnificent premises of the Giza Museum – namely at the monumental northern balcony – the examination of the mummies became an important social event attended by prestigious visitors[79] and archaeologists, including Maspero, Grébaut and Émile Brugsch (former assistant curator at the Bulak Museum) (Figs 9 and 10).

A vast number of objects were cleared from the mummy wrappings, thus extending considerably the collection of antiquities found in *Bab el-Gasus*. The report published by Daressy in 1907 provides a vast list of objects found during the examination of the mummies, which is still the most valuable tool for understanding the original composition of the burial assemblages. Daressy and Fouquet started their examination by opening the coffins, where they sometimes found a variety of objects, including sandals[80] and shoes,[81] garments,[82] cloths, and wigs.[83] Also in this context, Daressy found a whip[84] and a box containing magical objects.[85]

The mummies were usually wrapped in a shroud decorated with a large sketch depicting Osiris and bearing the name and titles of the deceased, or even a reference to the High Priest or the king under whose orders the mummification had been executed or restored. The mummy braces, either found bend over the mummy itself or on its outer wrappings, are also precious sources for this kind of historical information. Nearly 50 mummies provided this type of historical reference. High Priest Pinedjem II is the most frequently quoted (23 mummies), followed by Menkheperre (11 mummies) and Psusennes (10

---

74 Daressy, *Annales du Service des Antiquités de l'Égypte* 1, p. 144.
75 The number of mummycovers was not estimated by Daressy and its exact number is still uncertain but at least 60 mummycovers have been identified until now.
76 Once in the Museum, the objects would receive a fourth serial number, the *Catalogue Géneral* numbers.
77 Daressy, *Révue Archaeologique* 3, p. 73.
78 See Daressy, *Révue Archaeologique* 3, pp. 72-73.
79 On the occasion of the examination of the mummy from A.91, on 14 February 1902 Daressy reports several prestigious visitors, including Mr. and Mrs. Keatinge, Sir Frederick Treves and Lady Treves, Major Ratcliffe, Mr. Ruffer and M. E. Naville (G. Daressy, 'Procès verbal d'ouverture de la momie n° 29707', *Annales du Service des Antiquités de l'Égypte* 3 (1902), p. 151). Later, in the premises of the Cairo Egyptian Museum, Sir Eldon Gorst and Miss Gorst, S.E. Pinching, Professor Keatinge and his wife, Professor Elliot Smith and his wife, Dr. Fouquet and his wife, M.P. Lacau, Madame Kramer and her daughter were present at the examination which took place on 12 May 1903 (G. Daressy, 'Ouverture des momies provenant de la Seconde Trouvaille de Deir el-Bahari', *Annales du Service des Antiquités de l'Égypte* 4 (1903), p. 150).
80 A.50, A.72, A.127, A.129.
81 A.66, A.72, A.83.
82 A.72.
83 A.72, A.17, A.116.
84 A.24.
85 A.83, A.127.

Figure 9: Examination of a Mummy of the Priestess of Ammon (1891). Oil on canvas, by Paul Dominique Philippoteaux. Photo credit: Peter Nahum at The Leicester Gallery, London. Fouquet is depicted at the centre, with Grébaut at his right and Daressy on his left, taking notes. Other Egyptologists witness to the examination: Brugsch, Bazil, Barois and Bouriant.

mummies). The Tanite kings Siamon and Psusennes II were both mentioned only once.[86] This finding demonstrates once again the relative political independence of the High Priests at Thebes, following their own genealogy rather than that of the kings from Tanis. 46 coffins contained a papyrus scroll with funerary texts. These were usually placed between the legs of the mummy and sometimes on the chest,[87] around the abdomen,[88] or legs.[89] One coffin revealed three papyri, an exceptional find.[90] The amulets found in the mummies varied considerably. In the simplest burials, the mummy was merely equipped with a wax tablet decorated with the *udjat*-eye[91] and the

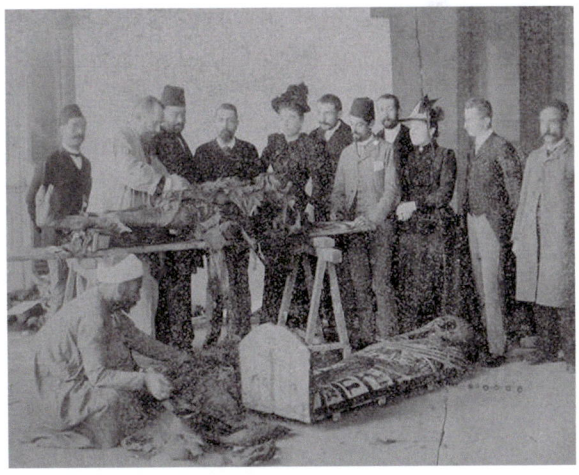

Figure 10: Examination of a mummy by Fouquet. Grébaut is standing at his left and Daressy figures on the top of the table, taking notes.

---

86   See R. Sousa, 'O Portal dos Sacerdotes: Uma leitura compreensiva do espólio de Bab el-Gassus', *Cadmo* 21 (2011), p. 85.
87   A.81, A.98, A.127.
88   A.113, A.127, A.150.
89   A.152.
90   A.127.
91   *Udjat*-plaques were found in nearly 45 mummies. See Sousa, *Cadmo* 21, p. 85.

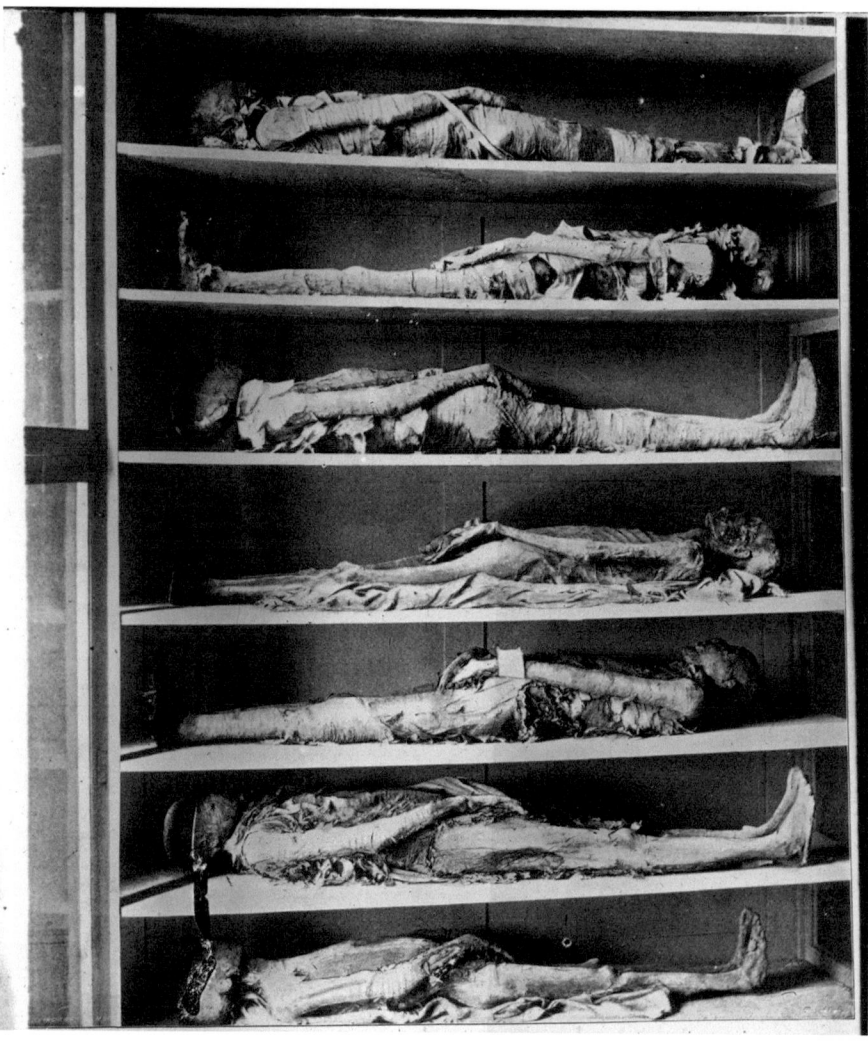

Figure 11: Showcase with a sample of unwrapped mummies from Bab el-Gasus at the Giza Museum (Room 85/86).

heart scarab.[92] Other items were included in more luxuriously equipped burials, such as the heart amulet,[93] a falcon-shaped pectoral (usually in gilded bronze or copper),[94] sacred cobras,[95] golden necklaces, gilded pectorals,[96] bracelets,[97] golden rings,[98] and earrings.[99] Small collections of amulets were sometimes found on the throat.[100]

At least 18 mummies were equipped with wax figurines depicting the four Sons of Horus. Sometimes the researchers also found *shabtis* inside the mummy.[101]

---

92 Heart scarabs were found in nearly 43 mummies. See Sousa, *Cadmo* 21, p. 85.
93 Heart amulets were found in at least nine mummies. Sousa, *Cadmo* 21, p. 85.
94 This type of pectoral was found in 19 mummies. Sousa, *Cadmo* 21, p. 85.
95 Three occurrences were reported, normally on the forehead (A.85, A.98, A.127 e A.151).
96 Two occurrences were reported (A.50, A.139), one with golden beads (A.50) and the other composed of small amulets (A.139).
97 Three occurrences were reported (A.50, A.133, A.139).
98 A.50, A.83.
99 A.50.
100 A.65, A.84, A.125.
101 In A.32. See E. Smith, 'An account of the mummy of a priestess of Amen supposed to be Ta-usert-em-suten-pa', *Annales du Service des Antiquités de l'Égypte* 7 (1906), pp. 155-160.

In addition, a large number of floral garlands were recorded by Daressy[102] and most interestingly bulbs under the feet and hands.[103] He also reported the use of mud sprinkled with seeds,[104] possibly resulting from a regeneration ritual comparable to the concept of corn mummies, and wax, as a sealing mainly of the eye-lids.[105]

On the mummies themselves, Daressy supplies little information (Fig. 11). We know from his registers that many of them were reduced to a skeleton.[106] According to his records, elderly people were rare in the community buried in *Bab el-Gasus*. Only one old woman is explicitly referred to in his report,[107] as well as a hunchback man.[108]

Among the mummies found in *Bab el-Gasus*, many of them revealed a premature death, usually before the age of twenty,[109] some even as children.[110] It is interesting to note the occurrence of a dual burial of a woman and her child (A.83), which is an exceptional occurrence in the Egyptian archaeology, where the autonomy of the burials is strictly observed, with the corpses kept in separate coffins.

3.4.2 After 1903 – Unwrappings at the Egyptian Museum in Cairo

A report dating from 1902 makes clear that the examination of the mummies was still in progress in the Giza Museum.[111] However, after the first examination in Giza, the mummies were now sent to the Medical School in Cairo[112] to complete the process. By 1903, the examination of the mummies carried out by Daressy and G. Elliot Smith was already taking place in the new premises of the Egyptian Museum in Cairo.[113] The increasing input of medical knowledge is clear from these reports.[114] The examination of the mummies produced by Elliot Smith is much more detailed in terms of the mummification procedures and anatomical considerations.[115] Thanks to him, we now know that

"there is no uniformity in the treatment of the viscera nor in the placing of the organs or the wax figures. Sometimes the organs are wrapped up; in other cases they are uncovered; in some cases the intestines are rolled together in one mass, in other cases they are cut into long straight pieces the ends of which are tied with string ; each organ may be placed in any situation : the wax or pottery figures may be with the viscera or may be placed apart ; and finally the figures are not associated with the same viscera in different mummies." [116]

The picture provided by the examination of the mummies reveals that the community of individuals buried in *Bab el-Gasus*, the elite of the Theban society of this period, was very heterogeneous, including both humble and luxury burials, most of them youngsters. Unfortunately, the location of these mummies is now lost. The massive removal of antiquities from the Giza Palace to the Egyptian Museum at Kasr el-Nil played another part in the increasing uncertainty surrounding the current location of the mummies. Recent research carried out by Salima Ikram has located a large amount of human remains in the storerooms of the Egyptian Museum, most of them reduced to bones and packed together, which are likely to belong to the mummies found in *Bab el-Gasus*. A few unwrapped mummies have also been located.

It is also quite possible that a good number of the currently unallocated artefacts were sold by the authorities during the period from 1904 to 1909 and it is likely that some of them are yet to be discovered in private and museum collections. The mummy and case in the Albany Institute of History and Art is one example of this, having arrived from Egypt in 1909.[117]

All in all, the report published in 1907 by Daressy contains the results of the examination of 93 coffin sets. However, Daressy does not provide any explanation of why the findings in the missing 60 burial assemblages were never reported.

Moreover, Daressy's notes include discreet yet disturbing mention of the conditions surrounding the unwrapping of the mummies. When listing the results of the examination of the mummy of Hory (A.143), he states that *"le démaillotement n'a pas été términé"*, without referring to the reasons for such an unexpected and awkward occurrence.[118] Apparently, the archaeologist's work was conditioned by the interference of the authorities and

---

102 A.66, A.72, A.77, A.116, A.127, A.134, A.148, A.151.
103 A.82, A.120, A.151, A.127.
104 A.129.
105 A.133.
106 A.6, A.25.
107 A.133.
108 A.35.
109 A.20, A.50, A.127.
110 A.3, A.7, A.129, A.145, A.153.
111 The mummy under examination belonged to the coffin set A.91 but by that time the coffins had already been expedited to Berlin (Daressy, *Annales du Service des Antiquités de l'Égypte* 3, p. 151).
112 Daressy, *Annales du Service des Antiquités de l'Égypte* 3, p. 153. This procedure might explain the current difficulty in discovering the location of most of the mummies.
113 E. Smith, 'Report on the four mummies', *Annales du Service des Antiquités de l'Égypte* 4 (1903), pp. 156-160.
114 Smith, *Annales du Service des Antiquités de l'Égypte* 7, pp. 156-182.
115 Daressy, *Annales du Service des Antiquités de l'Égypte* 4, pp. 150-155; Smith, *Annales du Service des Antiquités de l'Égypte* 7, pp. 155-182.

116 Daressy, *Annales du Service des Antiquités de l'Égypte* 4, pp. 159-160.
117 Case of Ankhefenmut (Albany Institute of History & Art, Gift of Samuel W. Brown, 1909.18.1b). See P. Lacovara and S. D'Auria, *The Mystery of the Albany Mummies*, Albany 2016.
118 Daressy, *Annales du Service des Antiquités de l'Égypte* 8, pp. 36-37.

this factor perhaps explains not only the disappearance of some objects as the confusing management of the data concerning this find.[119]

3.5 The Dispersal of the Find

In 1892, Jacques de Morgan was appointed Director of the Service of Antiquities, replacing Eugène Grébaut, who was forced to resign following numerous complaints from both political and diplomatic quarters as well as from scholars.[120] The appointment of De Morgan, an engineer – instead of an Egyptologist – was a political compromise, aiming to keep the French Directorate of the Service of Antiquities under the British occupation of Egypt.[121]

At this moment, the diplomatic agenda of the period would play a decisive role in the ultimate fate of the antiquities found in *Bab el-Gasus*, namely during the coronation feast for the Khedive Abbas II Hilmy. The crowded conditions at the Giza Museum – bearing in mind that this wonderful palace now contained 254 newly arrived coffins just one year after its opening in 1890 – was the pretext for offering a portion of this find to the representatives of the diplomatic missions present in Cairo for the festivities.[122] As a result, a selection of the *Bab el-Gasus* coffins was retained for the Giza Museum and the rest of the objects were divided into groups each containing 4 or 5 coffins, nearly 90 *shabtis* and one or two *shabti*-boxes. The ambassadors then drew lots to determine who would be awarded which group of coffins.[123]

In the Giza Museum the preparation for shipment of the lots seems to have occurred without a qualified supervision and a number of mistakes occurred. As a result, objects from the same coffin set became separated. In other cases, last minute changes meant that objects that were supposed to stay in Cairo were included in the lots offered to the diplomats, such as the burial assemblage of Djedmutiuesankh (A.110) which, for unknown reasons, was sent to Lisbon instead.

In 1893 these lots were sent to the 17 countries involved in this diplomatic operation, including the Netherlands (see also chapter 4).[124] During the year 1893, the Foreign Lots reached their destinations. Originally seventeen museums profited from the Khedive's gift, but subsequently the coffins were reallocated. Once more, diplomacy would play an important role in the further dispersal of the collection, with these antiquities being used to reinforce political alliances or display the power of a particular regime. In Scandinavia, for instance, king Oscar II decided to divide Lot XIV between Sweden and Norway, which were still joined in a political union.[125] Lot VI would be drastically dispersed throughout the vast territory of the URSS.[126] In the Swiss territory, Lot IX was divided to allow several cantons an equal share of the collection.[127] The French Lot is also one of the most scattered of the find. Today at least 35 museums are known to house objects from *Bab el-Gasus*.

For more than a century, the dispersed find of *Bab el-Gasus* witnessed the changing political and historical circumstances that affected most of the nations involved in this diplomatic operation. The collapse of the colonial empires, the two World Wars and the Cold War redefined the political map of Europe, Asia and the Middle East. This rapid succession of events played a major part in ensuring that collections lay forgotten, in most cases consigned to storerooms. It would take more than a century before this scattered collection began to be recognised as one of the major achievements of the Egyptian archaeology.

3.6 The Future of the Find

It is fair to acknowledge the tenacious effort by Georges Daressy in the patient documentation of the find under unbelievably difficult circumstances. With all its errors and mistakes, the records published by Daressy not only prevented its complete oblivion as became the fundamental basis for the modern reconstruction of the find. The

---

119 Another intriguing fact pointed out by Andrzej Niwiński is that three of the most important burial assemblages were never given Catalogue General numbers (see J. Lipinska, 'Bab el-Gusus: Cache-tomb of the priests & priestesses of Amen', *KMT* 4 (1993-1994), pp. 48-60). They were the cases of Hory (A.143), his sister Gatseshen, and an anonymous priestess, the daughter of a high-priest. In the latter case, only the outer lid has been preserved, while the outer coffer and the inner coffer and cover are missing. See Lipinska, *KMT* 4, pp. 48-60.

120 C. Orsenigo, 'Turning Points in Egyptian Archaeology (1850-1950)', in: P. Piacentini (ed.), *Egypt and the Pharaohs: From the Sand to the Library – Pharaonic Egypt in the Archives and Libraries of the Università degli Studi di Milano*, Milan 2010, p. 132.

121 Orsenigo, 'Turning Points', p. 132.

122 Lipinska, *KMT* 4, pp. 48-60.

123 Lipinska, *KMT* 4, pp. 48-60.

124 Lot I (France), Lot II (Austria), Lot III (Turkey), Lot IV (United Kingdom), Lot V (Italy), Lot VI (Russia), Lot VII (Germany), Lot VIII (Portugal), Lot IX (Switzerland), Lot X (USA), Lot XI (Netherlands), Lot XII (Greece), Lot XIII (Spain), Lot XIV (Sweden-Norway), Lot XV (Belgium), Lot XVI (Denmark), Lot XVII (Vatican).

125 A. Bettum, 'Lot XIV from Bab el-Gasus (Sweden and Norway): The modern history of the collection and a reconstruction of the ensembles', in: R. Sousa (ed.), *Body, Cosmos and Eternity: New Research Trends in the Iconography and Symbolism of Ancient Egyptian Coffins*, Oxford 2014, pp. 167-186.

126 M. Tarasenko, 'The Third Intermediate Period coffins in the museums of Ukraine', A. Amenta and H. Guichard (eds), *Proceedings of the First Vatican Coffin Conference*, Rome 2017, pp. 529-540.

127 A. Küffer and R. Siegman, *Unter dem Schutz der Himmelsgöttin: Ägyptische Särge, Mumien und Masken in der Schweiz*, Zürich 2007.

systematic study of the extraordinary documental corpus found in *Bab el-Gasus* is revealing outstanding insights into one of the most obscure periods of the Egyptian history. Modern examination of these antiquities reveals that a fair amount of its 153 burials were previously kept in other funerary grounds of the necropolis and were later on taken to *Bab el-Gasus*,[128] involving, as Kathlyn Cooney has been thoroughly demonstrating, the intensive and unprecedented re-use of funerary goods[129] (see also chapter 6). The burials of 153 priests and priestesses of Amun found in *Bab el-Gasus* are thus dated from different moments of the 21st Dynasty and provide a transversal coop on the community of the priests of Amun, the Theban elite of this period, which is an exceptional circumstance in the Egyptian archaeology.[130]

Besides the find, the tomb itself has known a similar story of oblivion and neglect. In fact, after the clearance of the Amun priests' tomb was completed in February 1891, the shaft was again filled up with the debris Grébaut had removed and it remained inaccessible until reopened in 1924 by Herbert Winlock of the Metropolitan Museum of Art. Winlock subsequently used the empty corridors of the tomb as a magazine for the storage of artifacts found during in the excavations he directed at Deir el-Bahari.[131]

Later on the shaft became refilled with debris and it was not until 1969 that the Polish Mission at Deir el-Bahari opened the tomb once more. Ten years later, in 1979, the Egyptian Antiquities Organization granted the Polish Mission permission to use the empty tomb for storing finds being made in the thoroughly ruined Thutmose III temple at Deir el-Bahari.[132] At that time a plan was made by the architect Rafal Czedner, which is so far the most updated plan of the tomb,[133] which remains inaccessible for visitors and researchers.

The undecorated character of the tomb, certainly played a major role in the almost complete neglect of its exceptional features. After all, it was built after a long period of intensive recycling and re-use of funerary structures and it reveals a turning point in the pattern of occupation of the Theban necropolis. Until the pontificate of the High Priest Pinedjem II (990-969 BCE), the necropolis was used as a network of small caches installed in re-used tombs managed by the priesthood of Amun. With *Bab el-Gasus* a totally different phenomenon emerges: the excavation of a new funerary site designed from the start to be used as a collective burial ground of the priesthood of Amun (see also chapter 2). The historical antecedent of this type of funerary site is to be found in the tomb of the sons of Ramesses II (KV 5),[134] which literally held the brotherhood of the sons of the king. It is therefore interesting to relate the creation of this new type of burial ground with a new ideological definition of the status and identity of the priests of Amun. As a collective tomb, *Bab el-Gasus* reveals a new understanding of this community as a ritual 'brotherhood' of men and women serving under the theocratic rule of Amun, the 'king of gods'.[135] More clues of these representations can actually be detected in coffin decoration dating from this period. The stylistic heterogeneity of the coffins reveals the use of sophisticated methods by the Theban workshops aiming to produce complex objects conveying a multi-layered system of messages that encoded representations of status, religious beliefs and ritual knowledge that were nuclear to the collective identity of the priesthood of Amun.[136] Despite the hazardous circumstances that surrounded this discovery and its subsequent dispersion, *Bab el-Gasus* presents unrivalled opportunities and challenges our global civilization to use scientific and technological resources to overcome the obstacles created by its dispersion. With outstanding documental corpora yet largely to be explored, *Bab el-Gasus* undoubtedly figures as one of the most important landmarks of the Egyptian archaeology.

---

128 Niwiński, *21st Dynasty Coffins*, p. 26.
129 E.g. K. Cooney, 'Ancient Egyptian funerary arts as social documents: social place, reuse, and working towards a new typology of 21st Dynasty coffins', in: R. Sousa (ed.), *Body, Cosmos and Eternity: New Research Trends in the Iconography and Symbolism of Ancient Egyptian Coffins*, Oxford 2014, pp. 45-66.
130 The burial chambers hold the most important funerary assemblages, those of the members of the families of the high-priests of Amun. The transversal gallery seems to have been used to hold the priests of higher rank while the main gallery seems to have been filled in with visibly humble burials, most of them used as part of the blocking system itself.
131 Lipinska, *KMT* 4, p. 56.
132 Lipinska, *KMT* 4, p. 56.
133 Lipinska, *KMT* 4, pp. 52-53.
134 K. Weeks, *The Lost Tomb: The Greatest Discovery at the Valley of the Kings Since Tutankhamun*, London 1999, pp. 240-241.
135 R. Sousa, 'Spread your wings over me: Iconography, symbolism and meaning of the central panel on yellow coffins', in: R. Sousa (ed.), *Body, Cosmos and Eternity: New Research Trends in the Iconography and Symbolism of Ancient Egyptian Coffins*, Oxford 2014, p. 107.
136 Sousa, 'Spread your wings', p. 107.

Chapter 4

The Coffins in Leiden

Liliane Mann, Christian Greco, and Lara Weiss

4.1 The Letters of Willem Pleyte *(by Liliane Mann)*[137]

4.1.1 Introduction

Today the coffins from the *Bab el-Gasus* cache are located in at least 35 countries including the Netherlands (see also chapter 3). The story of how the Netherlands received part of this cache is the story of an observant director of the *Rijksmuseum van Oudheden* (commonly abbreviated to RMO) in Leiden. Due to his attentiveness and persistence the RMO possesses nowadays six coffins, three mummy boards, two *shabti*-boxes and 92 *shabtis* of this famous cache.[138]

In 2013, during the preparation of the exhibition "Coffins of the Amun Priests" in the RMO in collaboration with the *Musei Vaticani* and the Louvre in Leiden, several copies of letters of Willem Pleyte (director of the museum from 1891 until 1903) concerning the *Bab el-Gasus* cache were discovered. Pleyte's letters revealed that due to his involvement, Leiden received Lot XI from the *Bab el-Gasus* cache. However, this was not the original plan of the Egyptian Government in 1893 when they decided to raffle off part of the cache.[139] The letters discovered in the RMO revealed that Pleyte was in contact with the Dutch Ministry of Foreign Affairs, the curators of the museum and the representative of the Dutch government in Cairo, the honorable Pieter Joseph Frans Marie van der Does de Willebois.[140] Additionally, the letters written by director Pleyte give an impression of the relationship between the European countries and Egypt. Willem Pleyte was born in Hillegom in 1836. He wanted to become a pastor like his father. For this purpose he studied theology in Utrecht from 1855-1860, but during the two years he spent waiting in vain for an appointment as pastor, he decided to pursue his studies now focusing on Egyptology.[141] Among other things, Pleyte studied the important papyri in the *Museo Egizio* in Turin, Italy. Together with Francesco Rossi, the curator of the *Museo Egizio*, he published part of the papyri and made them accessible for a larger public.[142] In 1869

---

137 See also L. Mann, 'The Letters of Willem Pleyte', in: A. Amenta and H. Guichard (eds), *Proceedings of the First Vatican Coffin Conference*, Rome 2017, pp. 289-292.
138 See Leiden Inv. no. F93/10.1-98 and Aston, *Burial Assemblages*, pp.164-198.
139 C. Greco et. al, *De reis van de kisten. Mummiekisten van de Amon-priesters,* Leiden 2013, p. 14.
140 See *Nationaal Archief,* no. *Archiefinventaris* 2.05.133.
141 H. Hasselbach, 'Bibliografie van W. Pleyte', *Oudheidkundige Mededelingen uit het Rijksmuseum van Oudheden* 67 (1987), pp. 93-99 and P.A.A. Boeser, 'Levensbericht van Dr. W. Pleyte', *Handelingen en Mededeelingen van de Maatschappij der Nederlandsche Letterkunde te Leiden, over het jaar 1910-1911*, Leiden 1904, pp. 91-112.
142 Boeser, 'Levensbericht', p. 98.

he applied for a job as curator at the RMO in Leiden but was refused the position due to the opposition from the then director of the museum, Conradus Leemans. However, after directing his application for the job to the Dutch Government, Leemans had to take him on anyway. It is noteworthy that Leemans appointed him as curator of the Dutch and Classical Department instead of the Egyptology Department, but ultimately, following the retirement of Leemans in 1891, Pleyte became the director of the RMO. He brought many improvements, among those the reorganization and expansion of the museum. According to Boeser, Pleyte was a versatile archaeologist, and apart from being an excellent Egyptologist a good classicist and well aware of the Dutch archaeology.[143] Early in the year 1903 he had to take his leave because of his poor health and passed away a few weeks later.

4.1.2 The Letters

In the beginning of 1893, an article appeared in a Dutch national newspaper[144] concerning the plan of the Egyptian government to raffle off part of the *Bab el-Gasus* cache to the six major European powers of that time – The Vatican, Austria-Hungary, England, the Prussian Empire, Russia and France – for their museum collections.

After reading this article, Pleyte sent one of his curators, Henri Jean de Dompierre de Chaufepié,[145] to the Dutch Minister of Foreign Affairs, Gijsbert van Tienhoven,[146] to find out if the RMO had a chance to obtain a part of the *Bab el-Gasus* cache. After the meeting of De Dompierre and the Minister of Foreign Affairs, Pleyte wrote his first letter to the minister.[147] In this letter from 11 March 1893 Pleyte asked minister van Tienhoven for the assistance of the Dutch government in obtaining part of the *Bab el-Gasus* cache for the museum. In his opinion, Pleyte had some solid arguments in order to qualify for a share of the cache: the already existing Egyptian collection of the RMO and the yearly publications (*Monumens Égyptiens du Musée d'Antiquités des Pays-Bas à Leide*) sent by the museum to the Egyptian government since Caspar Reuvens, the first director of the Leiden museum and a contemporary of Champollion, were sufficient reasons to legitimise his claim. Furthermore, he argued that although not belonging to the major European powers of that time, on an intellectual level the Netherlands and most certainly the museum in Leiden were quite able to compete with the powers referred to. His arguments must have persuaded the minister, because on that same day Van Tienhoven sent a letter to the representative of the Dutch government in Cairo, the honorable Pieter Joseph Frans Marie van der Does de Willebois, in which the minister asked Van der Does to represent the interests of the museum in Leiden in the upcoming distribution of the *Bab el-Gasus* cache. Ten days later, on 21 March, Van der Does sent his reply to the minister, wherein he wrote that steps had already been taken in favour of the RMO. Van der Does believed that Leiden had a fair chance of getting part of the cache, with preference however, going to the original six countries considered as was customary in all political or non-political matters.[148]

---

143 Boeser, 'Levensbericht', pp. 99 and 106.
144 Unfortunately, I have not found the article Pleyte must have read in the beginning of 1893, but it must be a text with the same content as the text found in the Dutch newspaper '*Nieuws van de Dag*', 14 March 1893: '*Verdeling over zes mogendheden (Londen, Parijs, Berlijn, Wenen, St Petersburg, Rome)*' (cf. http://kranten.kb.nl/view/text/id/ddd%3A010091811%3Ampeg21%3Ap001%3Aa0096, accessed on 17 March 2017).
145 Mr. de Dompierre was in the service of the RMO during a short period of time. In March 1892 De Dompierre was appointed as curator in the RMO. He left the RMO already in 1893 to return to the Royal Numismatic Collection to succeed its former director, cf. A.A. Looyen, *Jaarboek van de Maatschappij der Nederlandse Letterkunde* 1911, pp. 127-128.
146 Dutch Minister of Foreign Affairs from 21 August 1891 until 21 March 1894 (see *Parlement en Politiek*, https://www.parlement.com/id/vg09llapvtyj/g_van_tienhoven, accessed on 17 March 2017).
147 11 March 1893, Inv. No. 58 Out., Archive Box 17.01.01/48.
148 Inv. No. 187/44 In., Archive Box no. 17.01.01/39.

On 20 April 1893, Pleyte received a letter from the curators of the University of Leiden.[149] Enclosed were two appendices. One appendix turned out to be a letter of Van der Does with a follow-up of his previous letter (dated 21 March 1893), describing his meeting with the Egyptian Minister of Foreign Affairs, Mr. Tigram Pacha. Tigram Pacha had advised Van der Does to send him an official letter referring to the distribution of the Egyptian gift in which he explained the interests of the RMO. According to Tigram Pacha, it was important that Van der Does mentioned the yearly publications sent by the Dutch museum to the Egyptian government in this letter to emphasise the already existing connection between the Dutch museum and Egypt. After Van der Does did as instructed, Tigram Pacha had replied that he promised to serve the interests of the Dutch museum.

On 16 May, the Dutch Ministry of Foreign Affairs wrote a letter to the Dutch Ministry of Home Affairs to confirm that the RMO in Leiden would indeed receive part of the *Bab el-Gasus* cache.[150]

The raffle[151] of the *Bab el-Gasus* objects finally took place in Giza on 10 June, as stated in a letter of the curators of the University of Leiden dated 6 July 1893.[152] Pleyte received the aforementioned letter almost a month after the raffle had taken place. Five appendices were enclosed. One of the appendices was a further letter of Van der Does, informing the reader that the raffle had taken place in Giza. Leiden would receive Lot XI. In addition, he mentioned that the preparation of the lot for shipment to the Netherlands would take at least two months and would be executed by staff of the Antiquity Service in Cairo. The Egyptian Antiquity Service would also take on the costs of shipping. In one of the other appendices, also written by Van der Does, one could read that the collection was split up into two parts for the drawing of the lots: one part was, according to Van der Does, meant for the major powers and the other part for the so-called second-rate countries. Since he was able to see the collection in Giza, Van der Does was convinced that the major powers were favoured with more and better objects. However, the curators of the University of Leiden regarded Van der Does unqualified to make this judgement and thus did not attach much value to his remarks; the issue of how to thank the Egyptian government for the gift was considered much more important.

The three remaining appendices of the letter of 6 July 1893 contained an overview of the *Bab el-Gasus* objects intended for the RMO, but proved to be incomplete as only 46 *shabtis* were mentioned as opposed to the 92 currently in the Leiden collection. This list, written in French and not in Dutch as the other appendices, is probably a copy of the list of Émile Brugsch, who was working as an assistant curator in the Egyptian museum in Giza during that time.[153] It turned out that the lists of the *Bab el-Gasus* cache made by Brugsch[154] for France and the Netherlands mentions 46 *shabtis*. What is meant is probably 46 *shabti owners*. The total number of shabtis Leiden eventually received was 92[155].

In the autumn of 1893, on 11 October, another letter from the curators of the University of Leiden arrived at the RMO.[156] Enclosed was a letter from Mr. Pieter Charles van Lennep,[157] Deputy Representative of the Dutch government in Cairo, stating that six crates containing the Egyptian objects were on their way to the Netherlands on the steamer, 'Prins Alexander'. This ship belonged to the fleet of the *'Stoomvaartmaatschap-*

---

149 At that time, the *Rijksmuseum van Oudheden* was still part of the University of Leiden. For the letter see RMO letter archive, Inv. No. 244 In., Archive Box. no. 17.01.01/39.
150 Inv. No. 5339 In., Archive Box. no. 17.01.01/48.
151 See, for example, Niwiński, *21st Dynasty Coffins*, 1988, 26.
152 Inv. No. 423 In., Archive Box. no. 17.01.01/39.
153 A. Dautant *et al.*, 'Distribution and Current Location of the French Lot from the Bab el-Gasus Cache', Poster presentation at the First Vatican Coffin Conference, Rome, June 19-22, 2013.
154 A. Dautant *et al.*, 'Distribution and Current Location'.
155 Dautant *et al.* 2013, poster.
156 Inv. No. 618 In., Archive Box. no. 17.01.01/39.
157 See *Dutch Nationaal Archief, nummer Archiefinventaris* 2.05.133.

pij Nederland' and travelled between the Dutch East Indies and the Netherlands on a regular basis.[158] The ship with its valuable cargo arrived at the beginning of October 1893 in Amsterdam.

On 6 October of the same year, Pleyte wrote to the De Vries & Co, a stevedoring company, that the six crates sent by the Antiquity Service of Giza in Egypt and transported on the steamer 'Prins Alexander' should be forwarded to Leiden immediately without opening.[159] The crates would be inspected by officials upon arrival in Leiden. In his letter to De Vries & Co Pleyte described the expected contents of the crates, mentioning, as reported by the Egyptian authorities, four mummy cases, two *shabti*-boxes, and 46 *shabtis* – a total of 52 objects, worth 600 Dutch guilders.

Only six days later, on the 12 October, the cargo arrived in Leiden. Once the crates were opened, the following objects were revealed:

- Two sets of coffins, consisting of both an inner and an outer coffin and a mummy cover
- One inner coffin with a mummy cover
- One inner coffin
- Two *shabti*-boxes
- 92 *shabtis* (instead of the expected 46 *shabtis* as noted in the letter of 6 July 1893 and therefore cause of the misunderstanding)

On 19 October 1893, Pleyte informed the curators of the University of Leiden that the six crates with the Egyptian antiquities had arrived in Leiden noting that some of the objects were damaged. Among those one coffin that needed immediate restauration. Lack of space prevented Pleyte from unpacking the other coffins.[160]

Pleyte's last letter concerning the *Bab el-Gasus* cache was written on 15 November 1893. He wrote to the curators of the University of Leiden that the *Bab el-Gasus* coffins were restored and, as far as space permitted, were on display to the public. He called it '*A beautiful gift for which gratitude is expressed to the government*'[161] – whether he meant the Dutch or the Egyptian government is not clear.

The new acquisitions were registered in the inventory ledger of the museum. Pleyte noted that originally three of the lids must have been equipped with a gilded face that '*remarkably, at all three, is broken away, or stolen, or serving in the museum of Giza as an ornament*'.

In an interview with the Dutch daily newspaper '*De Tijd*' on 23 November 1893 Pleyte appeared more cheerful. He told the interviewer: '*Thanks to the friendly intervention of our minister van Tienhoven and our ambassador van der Does de Willebois we received a part* [of the *Bab el-Gasus* cache], *and, as I have noted, no less than England*'.[162] Pleyte could be satisfied; thanks to him, the RMO has received a major addition to its Egyptological collection.

---

158 https://www.geni.com/projects/Stoomvaart-Maatschappij-Nederland-1870-1970/3180, accessed on 12 January 2017.
159 Inv. No. 246 Out. Archive Box. no. 17.01.01/48.
160 Inv. No. 249 Out. Archive Box. no. 17.01.01/48.
161 Inv. No. 254 Out. Archive Box. no. 17.01.01/48.
162 Daily journal 'De Tijd', 17-03-1893, http://kranten.kb.nl/view/text/id/ddd%3A010407094%3Ampeg21%3Ap001%3Aa0105 accessed on 17 March 2017.

4.2 Lot XI in Leiden *(by Christian Greco and Lara Weiss)*

4.1.1 Introduction

In about a month after their arrival the coffins were restored. On 15 November 1893 Pleyte proudly announced that the new acquisitions were on museum display:

> *"The beautiful ('fraaie') gift consists of two whole and two parts of coffin sets from the XIX and XX dynasties [sic!][163], belonging to spiritual women who have held their office at the service of Amun and Mut, chief gods of Thebes. A set usually consists of a three coffins that fit in each other; and in the last of which the mummy. The first set belongs to Katses'ni. The mummy is missing as well as in the following [coffin]. The second [belongs] to Nesi-ta-neb-taui; of the third set we received the second coffin and the lid of the coffin or cartonage, having belonged to Tent-pen-hau-nofer. Of the fourth set, the name of the deceased is not attested. In addition, we received two boxes for shabti figurines, one of which attesting the name of the deceased Nes-Pa-Ka-s'uti. Finally 92 pieces of shabti figurines, of which several are important for [their] titles."*

The RMO indeed possesses the outer, middle and inner coffin of (what we know read as) Gautseshen (F 93/10.1a, -b, -c, Figs 12-14), the outer and inner coffin of Nesytanebtawy and her mummy board (F 93/10.2a, -b, c, Figs 15-17), the inner coffin and mummy board of Tjenetpenherunefer (F 93/10.3a, -b, Figs 18-19), an anonymous coffin (F 93/10.4, fig. 20), a *shabti*-box of Neskapashuty (F 93/10.5), an anonymous *shabti*-box ((F 93/10.6) and 92 *shabtis* ((F 93/10.7-98) (see also chapter 6). Yet the question of which coffins arrived in Leiden is a challenging one. In preparation of the 2013 exhibition in the RMO, Christian Greco compared the literature on the subject and observed some discrepancies.

---

163 Today we know that the coffins belong to the 21st Dynasty (see chapter 2).

Figure 12: Outer coffin of Gautseshen (Leiden inv. no. F 93/10.1a). Photo: RMO.

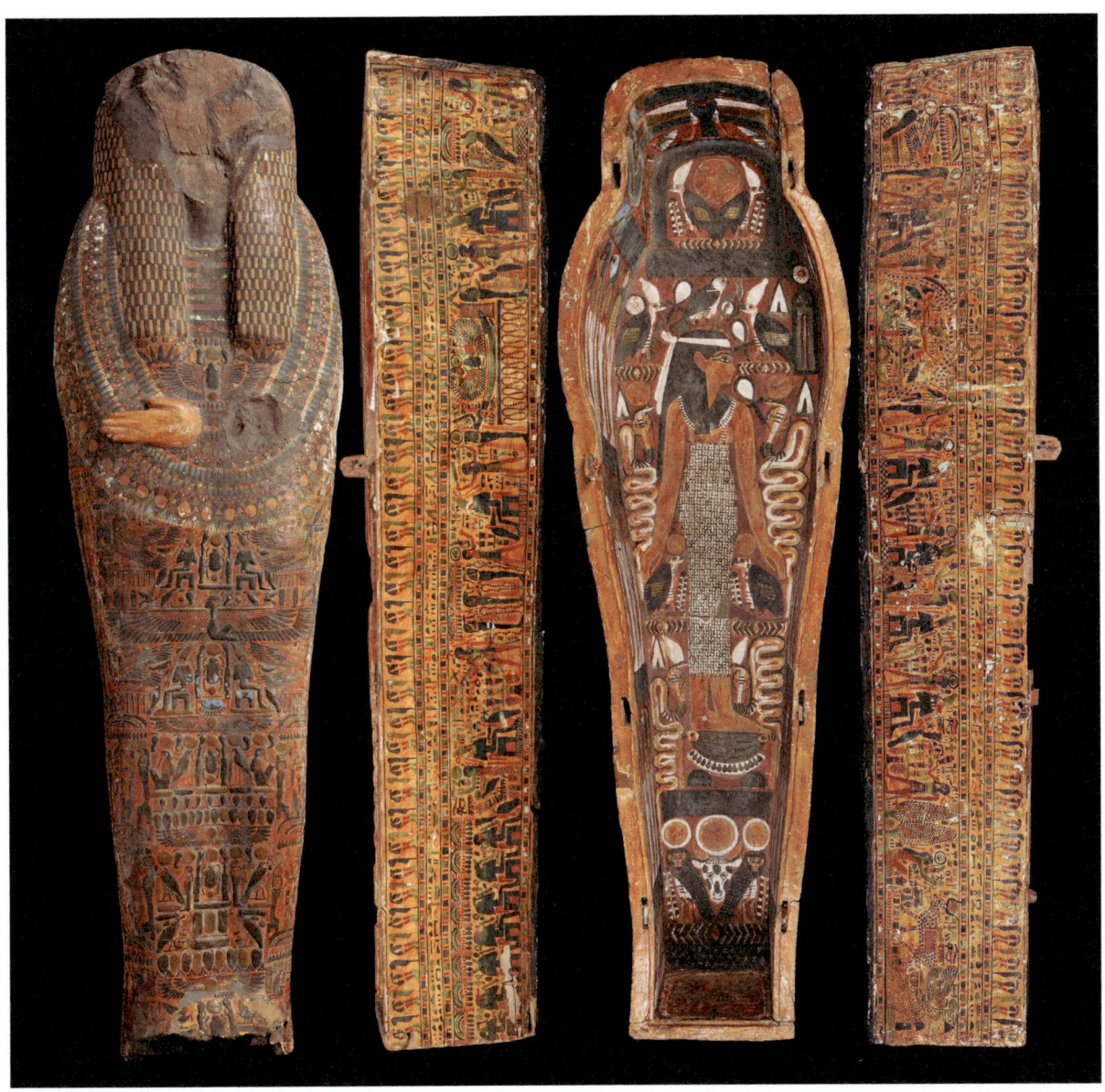

Figure 13: Inner coffin of Gautseshen (Leiden inv. no. F 93/10.1b).
Photo: RMO.

Figure 14: Mummy board of Gautseshen (Leiden inv. no. F 93/10.1c). Photo: RMO.

Figure 15: Outer coffin of Nesytanebtawy (Leiden inv. no. F 93/10.2a). Photo: RMO.

Figure 16: Inner coffin of Nesytanebtawy (Leiden inv. no. F 93/10.2b). Photo: RMO.

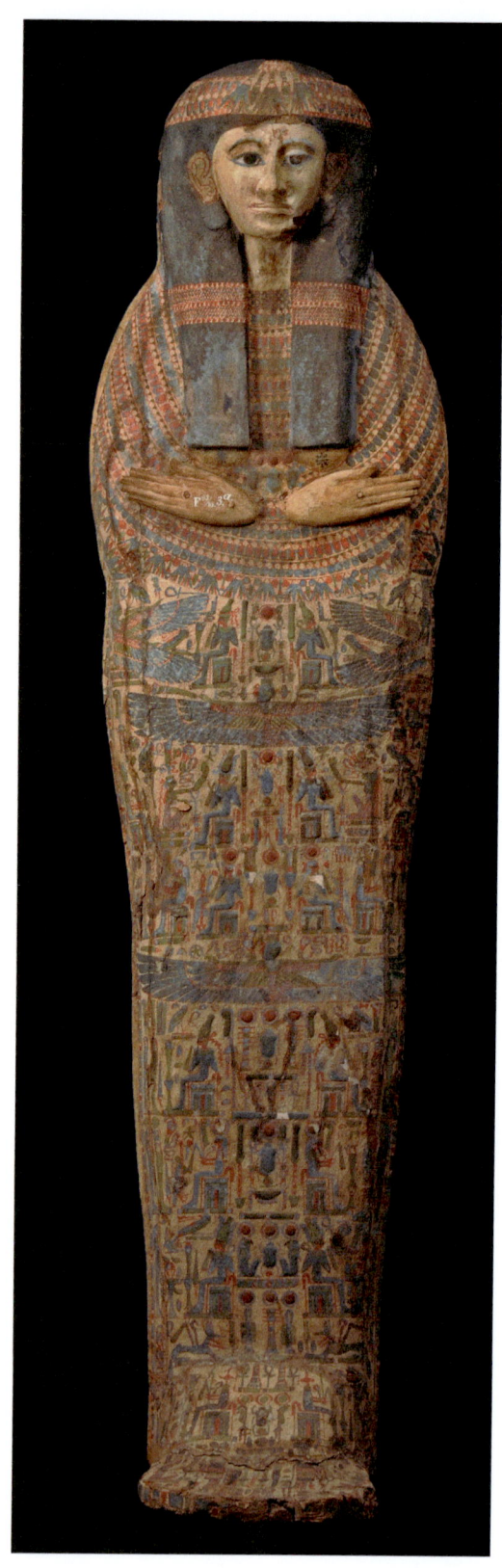

Figure 17: Mummy board of Nesytanebtawy (Leiden inv. no. F 93/10.2c). Photo: RMO.

Figure 18: Inner Coffin of Tjenetpenherunefer (Leiden inv. no. F 93/10.3a). Photo: RMO.

Figure 19: Mummy board of Tjenetpenherunefer (Leiden inv. no. F 93/10.3b). Photo: RMO.

Figure 20: Anonymous coffin (Leiden inv. no. F 93/10.4). Photo: RMO.

4.2.1 The Sources

We have seen (chapter 3) that when the coffins left the *Bab el-Gasus* cache they were numbered, and again when they arrived in Cairo. The numbers in the Daressy list are called A-numbers, whereas he calls the numbers Bouriant added to the coffins (when they left Luxor to be shipped to Cairo) B-numbers.[164] In his publication Daressy notes that the B-list is longer than the A-list because it lists also burial equipment and not only coffins. Arrived at Giza museum, the most attractive objects got *Journal d'Entrée* numbers. In addition Andrzej Niwiński published a catalogue of those coffins and numbered them again in 1988.[165] In 2009, the coffins received Aston TG (tomb group) numbers while these were again linked to the Daressy numbers.[166] During the preparations of the Leiden exhibition, Christian Greco found a French shipping list in the RMO archive that probably accompanied the coffins on their trip to Leiden. In the following the results of his research on the Leiden number problem shall be summarised.

4.2.2 The Leiden Number Problem

In order to check which coffins arrived in Leiden the shipping list appeared as a good starting point. The fact that it was written in French suggests that it could be a copy of the Egyptian shipping list compiled by Brugsch. The coffin of Gautseshen received number 39, but most probably this was a misspelling of 139. Yet the identification of the number of this coffin with our Leiden coffin remains somewhat controversial, because in fact, coffin A.139 should have remained in Cairo. According to Daressy, A.139 consisted of a coffins set belonging to Nesy-Imn-Tawy with a lid of a lady Gautseshen. On the Leiden set, the names and titles of Gautseshen are listed on the lid of the outer coffins, and on the foot board, whereas on the boxes only her titles are mentioned, which is odd. An explanation for the lack of names on the Leiden boxes is that the set was made for somebody else and then usurped by Gautseshen. It would be very unusual that that the name of the deceased would only be mentioned on the lid, but not the box itself. A closer examination of the hieroglyphic inscriptions by Christian Greco revealed that the name Gautseshen was written in a much thicker line than the rest of the text, suggesting that it was applied later, potentially on a still fresh varnish that made the paint running out a bit. Gautseshen's titles 'chantress of Amun' and 'chantress in the chamber (?) of the goddess Mut' are also attested there. With infrared reflectography Christian Greco and Elsbeth Geldhof tried to establish whether the empty spot on the box once showed a name, but nothing was seen unfortunately. Either a previously existing name had been removed without leaving any trace when the coffin was reused, or the coffin was mass-produced, i.e. constructed and decorated leaving an empty spot for the name of the future owner (and that this adding of the name never happened for whatever reason). At the foot board of the mummy cover the name Gautseshen and the titles 'chantress of Amun' and 'chantress in the chamber (?) of the goddess Mut' are yet again written in a way suggesting they were painted at the last minute on fresh varnish. However, since the name or Gautseshen is the only one on the set, it is not possible to identify any potential previous owner.

A second interesting discovery concerns the label that has been found on the rim of F 93/10.2a, belonging to the second set of coffins. The shipping list confirms this number. We can attest with certainty that the coffins in Leiden should correspond to the A list number 6, as correctly understood by Niwiński and Aston, and not to A.88, which remains in Cairo (seen by Rogério Sousa on display in the Cairo Tahir museum). The outer coffin identifies the owner of the coffin as Nesytanebtawy 'chantress of Amun'

---

164 Daressy, *Annales du Service des Antiquités de l'Égypte* 1, pp. 141-148; *Annales du Service des Antiquités de l'Égypte* 8, pp. 3-38; *Révue Archaeologique* 3, pp. 70-72; Niwiński, *Journal of Egyptian Archaeology* 70, pp. 73-80.
165 Niwiński, *21st Dynasty Coffins*, p. 26.
166 Aston, *Burial Assemblages*, pp. 164-198.

RMO inventory number	Name of the owner	Titles	Shipping list	Daressy	Niwiński	Aston	Identification
F 93/10.1	G'wtsšn	nb.t pr šm'y.t n 'Imn ḥsy.t n p3 ' n Mwt	39 (sic!) JE 29617	139	139		?
F 93/10.2	Nsy-t3-nb.(t)-t3wy	nb.t pr šm'y.t n 'Imn ḥsy.t n p3 ' n Mwt	29724	88	6	6	6
F 93/10.3	Tnt-pn-ḥrw-nfr	šm'y.t n 'Imn	47 (A list) 56 (B list)	47	47	47	47
F 93/10.4	anonymous		130 29741	130	?	130	?

Table 2: Numbers of the Leiden Coffins.

and 'chantress in the chamber (?) of the goddess Mut'. Clearly, the owner of the coffin was female, but the face shows a beard and no breasts have been moulded. Unfortunately, what would have been a clear indication of a male or female owner (namely the 'female' flat hands vs. 'male' clenched fist) is missing. Yet under the blue strokes of the wig the remains of red horizontal bands are still visible, a typical female headdress. Most probably this set was made for chantress Nesytanebtawy and later reused by a man (see also chapter 6). The inner coffin shows no traces of reuse. It does not attest any names or titles but it was clearly designed for a man. The question is whether the two coffins belonged together originally or whether they were combined by the second (male) owner.

As to F 93/10.3, the shipping list mentions the number 4756 which can easily be identified with the numbers 47 of the A-list and 56 of the B-list. The coffin belongs to Tjenetpenherunefer, yet another chantress of Amun. On the foot board the name of a w'b-priest called Di-Khonsu-iry is written in Hieratic script. This is in fact not a sign of reuse (contra Aston 2009, 172). Whereas Aston assigned A.47 to Di-Khonsu-iry and lists Tjenetpenherunefer as usurper, Di-Khonsu-iry was in fact part of the team responsible for the Wḥm-krs of the coffins, i.e. their reburial to protect them from plundering. That this was common practice is, for example, suggested by an hieroglyphic inscription of on the inside of a coffin now in the British Museum (BM 15659), which mentions the renewing the burial of a lady Tameniut.[167] Di-Khonsu-iry in fact appears also on a number of ostraca found in Dear el-Bahari, the Valley of the Kings, Medinet Habu, the Merenptah temple, and Deir el-Medina.

Finally, F 93/10.4, the fourth RMO inventory number of our group is an anonymous inner coffin. According to Daressy – who also notes it was anonymous – in the coffin a mummy Siamun was found, which identifies our Leiden coffin with A-list A 130.

---

167 Taylor, *Death and Afterlife*, p. 181. Reference kindly provided by Rob Demarée.

Chapter 5

Painting Techniques of the Leiden Coffins

Elsbeth Geldhof

5.1 Introduction
In 2011, the *Rijksmuseum van Oudheden* (RMO) joined the Vatican Coffin Project, and this was the starting point for extensive material analysis and paint investigation of the four *Bab el-Gasus* coffin sets in the collection of the RMO. In the autumn of that year, a pilot project started to investigate the potential scope and benefits of working collaboratively and interdisciplinary, combining the fields of Egyptology, Museology, Conservation, Conservation Science and Technical Art History.

The initial results of this interdisciplinary collaboration were presented at the 'Coffins of the Amun Priests' show in Summer 2013, which was organised by the *Rijksmuseum van Oudheden* in collaboration with specialists from the *Musée du Louvre* and the *Musei Vaticani*.[168] An important part of this exhibition was the display of the coffins and mummy boards of the four Leiden *Bab el-Gasus* coffin sets, within the setting of a conservation studio where treatments were performed in front of the public.

The research and conservation continued also after the exhibition. Paint research and material analysis was carried out following the Vatican Coffin Project Analysis Protocol.[169] This document describes the methods and instrumentation for technical imaging, non-invasive analysis and spot-sample analysis, to align the analysis standards at the institutions that are participating in the Vatican Coffin Project.

Analyses used for the identification of pigments, binding media and wood allow for collecting general data on the materials that were used for building and decorating the coffins. However, scientific analysis on itself cannot provide information about individual craftsmen, workshop methodologies or painting techniques. The study of painting techniques has to also rely on close observation (with the naked eye as well as a microscope), specialist imaging techniques and the investigation of the paint stratigraphy via paint cross section microscopy, additionally to the results of material analysis. Imaging techniques and close observation can also be used to investigate brush-marks, penmanship, and other tool-marks. This way, the under-drawing techniques and techniques to mark out the position of text bands and vignettes can be studied, the paint sequence can be investigated, and any changes originating from Antiquity as well as restoration interventions in more recent times can be identified.

---

168 See for the exhibition and preliminary results of the pilot project: Greco *et al.*, *Reis van de kisten*.
169 Amenta (ed.), *Analysis Protocol*.

5.2 Restoration History and Present-day Conservation Approach

In October 1893, four 21st Dynasty polychrome coffin sets of the *Bab el-Gasus* corpus arrived at the *Rijksmuseum van Oudheden* in Leiden, after excavation two years before and after a tremendous effort of the then museum director Pleyte to secure four coffin sets for the Leiden collection (see chapter 4).

The annual report for that year describes the arrival, and the immediate repair of the coffin sets, 15 objects in total, over the course of just one month before displaying them in the museum's Egyptian galleries (Fig. 21). The annual report also notes that one of the coffins had arrived badly damaged, and this might refer to the outer coffin of Nesytanebtawy which has been heavily repaired. These unspecified repairs were executed by a technical support person, a Mr. Koene, who later on went into the 'face books'[170] as the museum's plaster cast specialist – possibly an indication of what material (plaster) he felt comfortable working with for these repairs.

At the time, 'repair' meant performing some basic gluing and filling as one would have done with a broken piece of household furniture. Coincidentally, the earliest recognisable repairs on these coffin sets consist of plaster fills that mend gaps between planks, as well as textile strips that are glued to the underside of lids and coffins using a lead-white/linseed oil paste (a material unknown to ancient societies). These plaster fills and repairs with textile strips can therefore most likely be associated with the repairs mentioned in the museum's annual report of 1893. Unfortunately, over time, these repair materials have proven unsuitable for conservation because of their chemical instability and incompatibility with the wood, plaster layers and paint materials that the coffins were made of initially. This pulled the coffins in a circle of continuous repair. With every repair, more unsuitable material was added to the ancient object, often in a well-intended attempt to cover up discoloured or non-compatible materials from previous restoration treatments. As a result, the coffins and lids have undergone four (and in some cases even five) restoration treatments – all interventions that are having their impact on the current condition of the coffin sets.

It is not only these fairly recent interventions, that are distorting our view of the original, technical and material authenticity of the coffins' paintwork. The materials that the ancient craftsmen used may have deteriorated as well: the wood and textiles may be affected by insects, and chemical instability of pigments, binding media and varnishes may have resulted in a different colour or

Figure 21: A glimpse into the museum's Egyptian galleries around 1906. One of the Bab el-Gasus coffins (Gautseshen's outer coffin) is displayed in an upright position without additional support, in the case nearest to the viewer. Photo: RMO archive.

texture. Additionally, ongoing research into the re-purposing of coffins for a new owner is increasingly giving indications of recycling of materials, mixing up of coffin sets, and partial (or full) redecoration of coffins – all done in Antiquity. The coffin sets of *Bab el-Gasus* in particular were subject to extensive alterations due to changed ownership (see chapter 6). Interventions done in ancient as well as modern times, the change of location and climate, the continuous handling, the changes that are inherent to ancient materials as well as repair materials: all contribute to the current appearance. As a result, the objects we see in museums today are rarely quite the same as those originally put into the ancient Egyptian tombs.[171]

In the past decades, increased knowledge about the impact of active or passive interventions on artefacts as well as ongoing research into chemical and physical processes within art materials, has been instrumental for a changed perspective on the concepts of conservation, restoration and preservation. A current definition of conservation as 'the careful management of change' could therefore not be more accurate.[172] Following this definition, any conservation project requires a thorough knowledge of the object (or group of objects) and the changes they have gone through, to design and justify any new treatment. Such

---

170 A face book (in Dutch: '*smoelenboek*') is a (usually yearly produced) album with photos of all the personnel, from director to cleaners. The museum has several in their archives, the earliest dating from the late 19th century.

171 J. Dawson et al, 'Egyptian coffins: Materials, Construction and Decoration', in: *Death on the Nile. Uncovering the Afterlife of Ancient Egypt,* London 2016, p. 76.

172 See for this definition of the concept of conservation: English Heritage, *Conservation Principles, Policies and Guidance,* 2008, p. 74; Sarah Staniforth CBE, President of the International Institute of Conservation for Historic and Artistic Works (IIC), keynote lecture for the symposium at the occasion of the retirement of Professor Anne van Grevenstein-Kruse, University of Amsterdam 14 December 2011; Osterley Conservation Team Blog, The National Trust, osterleynationaltrust.wordpress.com (accessed 21 February 2017).

Figure 22: Detail of the outside of the inner coffin base of Tjenetpenherunefer F 93/10.3a. The pale colour that forms the background for the decoration and text, was initially meant as an opaque light yellow for which calcite, yellow ochre and orpiment were mixed in one paint layer. The orpiment has now lost its colour due to natural ageing processes that are inherent to the orpiment mineral. Photo: Elsbeth Geldhof.

a preliminary research can involve close observation, technical photography and other specialist imaging techniques, material analysis, wood technology, restoration history, and so on. For the four *Bab el-Gasus* coffin sets at the RMO, the preliminary research included the investigation of paint materials, painting tools and painting techniques, given their extensive restoration history, their high probability of ancient redecoration and their complex polychrome stratigraphy.

5.3 How Were the Leiden Coffins Painted?

The coffin sets of *Bab el-Gasus* [173] belong to a large group of polychrome coffins dating from the Third Intermediate Period. These are generally named 'yellow coffins' and their decoration is indeed characterised by a dominating brown or yellow hue that relates to either a yellow looking varnish, a yellow(-ish) background colour, or both. [174]

Some of the coffins carry a varnish on their multi-colour decoration, that has been applied in ancient times. Ancient varnish was made from natural resins, similar to picture varnishes on old master easel paintings. And just like varnished easel paintings, over the centuries of time these ancient varnishes also become yellow, brittle and opaque.

Additionally, many of the coffins have a distinct yellow background layer, that forms the backdrop for the decoration of texts and vignettes. Other coffins have a beige overall colour, either intentionally, or paler than it was originally due to degradation of an initially yellow pigment. Even a now *beige* coloured coffin (with or without a varnish) such as the inner coffin of Tjenetpenherunefer, F 93/10.3a, would still be referred to as a 'yellow coffin' (Figs 18 and 22).

---

173 The Bab el-Gasus coffin sets in the collection of the *Rijksmuseum van Oudheden* consist of: F 93/10.1a, -b, -c coffin set of Gautseshen, chantress of Amun: outer coffin, inner coffin and mummy board; F 93/10.2a, -b, -c coffin set of Nesytanebtawy, chantress of Amun: redecorated outer coffin and an inner coffin and mummy board for an anonymous man; F 93/10.3a, -b incomplete coffin set of a woman named Tjenetpenherunefer: inner coffin and mummy board; F 93/10.4 incomplete coffin set of an anonymous Priest of Amun: inner coffin.

174 The name 'yellow coffins' is a modern day convention, and is not (to our present knowledge) a term that has been used in ancient times to describe coffins from this type or period.

Figure 23: Fragment from the mummy board of Tjenetpenherunefer F 93/10.3b, showing the fine linen textile, and coarse brown-grey paste that once covered the complete mummy board. Photo: Elsbeth Geldhof.

Another characteristic of these type of coffins is their colourful, busy appearance that is enforced by a *horror vacui* decoration style. The complete surface, inside and out, is covered in text and vignettes with many figures, seemingly randomly placed elements such as eyes or wings, checked, striped, and dotted borders, and so on. All elements, whether it be text, decorative borders or figures, are built up in red, blue and green with details in black and white. The quality and skill of the crafts person who started the decoration by marking the general position of all these elements, was essential for the painting quality of the finished product. Something that would be misplaced in this 'marking-out' and under-drawing stage, could not easily be corrected by painters afterwards. This was because of the manner in which the polychrome decoration was built up. The decoration was not made in a painterly fashion, where a palette with all the colours would be available at any moment. Due to the high production of coffins in this period, and the use of expensive pigments that had to be imported, there was a need for efficiency and cost-effectiveness.[175] This was established by using pure, un-mixed pigments, one colour at the time, and by building up the decoration in a more or less standardised sequence. This sequence would start with applying preparation layers on the wood before starting with the actual decoration with marking-out lines, background colour, under-drawing, and filling-in of text and decoration with red, blue, and often green. This would be followed by small details in black and white. If the coffin, lid or mummy board was to receive a varnish, this would be applied last.

5.3.1 Materials and Their Application Sequence

In general, the materials of the painted surface form a complex layering where one material interacts with the other. The support for the polychrome decoration is wood, with textile on top. Presumably the textile would be applied over wood joins to bridge any irregularities. The more wood pieces were used to form a coffin base, lid or mummy board, the more likely it is that the textile has been applied over the complete surface

---

175 Cooney, *Cost of Death,* pp. 106-125.

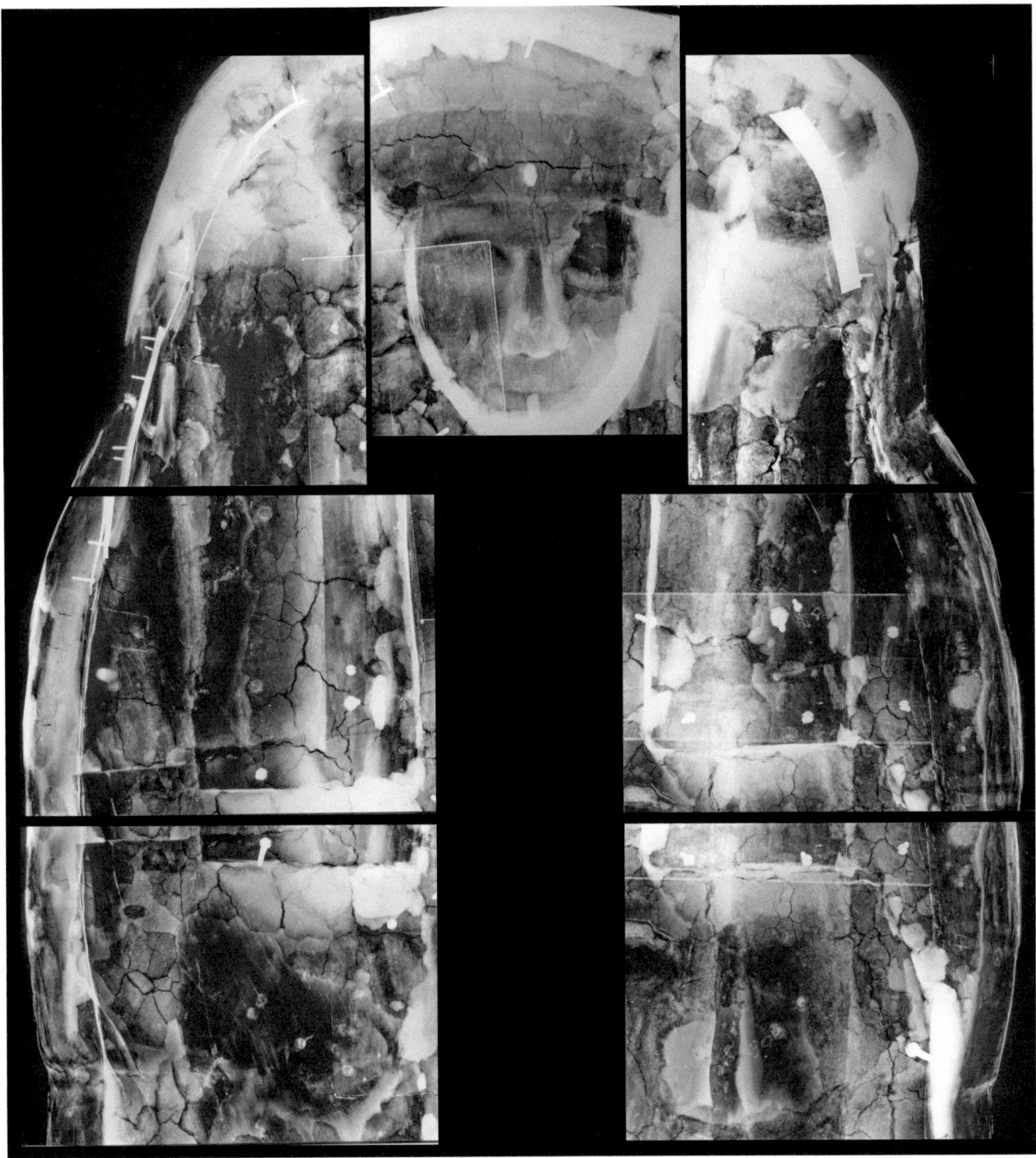

Figure 24: X-Radiograph of the head and chest area of the outer lid of Nesytanebtawy F 93/10.2a. Image: René Gerritsen, Amsterdam.

in order to create a homogenous, smooth surface that can support the polychrome decoration.

An overall layer of a coarse brown-grey paste was then placed over the textile patches, or on top of underneath an overall layer of textile, for example on the mummy board of Tjenetpenherunefer F 93/10.3b (Fig. 23).

The purpose of this coarse paste on the coffins seems to be similar to that on painted walls: to smooth out major irregularities,[176] although it was also used to build up wigs and free-form body features such as ears and breasts. Thick layers of brown-grey paste are

---

176 E. Miller, 'Painterly Technique', in: A. Middleton and K. Uprichard (eds), *The Nebamun Wall Paintings. Conservation, Scientific Analysis and Display at the British Museum,* London 2008, pp. 61-67, in particular p. 61.

PAINTING TECHNIQUES OF THE LEIDEN COFFINS | 53

Figure 25: Locally applied varnish on the heads of deities, on the inside of the outer coffin of Gautseshen F 93/10.1a. Photo: Elsbeth Geldhof.

particularly well visible on the x-radiograph of the head of the outer lid of the coffin of Nesytanebtawy F 93/10.2a (Fig. 24).[177]

The coarseness and colour of the paste is due to calcite, sand, clays, straw and wood fibers that are mixed in. In the literature, this type of paste is also very often referred to as 'mud layer' or 'mud plaster'[178]. This characterization is not that far off, considering the colour, and the shrinkage pattern on the radiograph that has the resemblance of a dried riverbed. The brown-grey paste received a finer, white paste layer, that serves as a preparation layer for the marking-out lines and under-drawing (which could be executed in red and/or black). The under-drawing could also be applied on top of the following yellow background layer(s). Here, on these four coffin sets, a second, brighter white layer has been applied for the collar areas on lids and mummy boards.

Then the red solid coloured areas were filled in, followed by application of the blue parts, the green, and finally details (such as eyes and beards of the figures in the vignettes) in black and white. The varnish would be applied last, if the coffin were to receive one.

The decorated inside of the coffins roughly followed the same colour sequence. The coffins of the sets of Gautseshen F 93/10.1a, -b and Nesytanebtawy F 93/10.2a, -b both have a similar inside decoration that received a partial varnish on key design elements, such as faces of deities (Fig. 25).

The sequence of layers and colours can be determined because of differences in thickness of the layers, helped by the fact that the variety of colours and pigments was extremely limited. The materials for the polychrome decoration on the Leiden *Bab el-Gasus* coffin sets and their application sequence with one colour at the time, is outlined in the table below. These findings are confirming René van Walsem's conclusions on the interior and exterior polychrome decoration of many Old Kingdom polychrome coffins.[179] Even though several centuries passed since the Old Kingdom, the colour sequence on these 21st Dynasty *Bab el-Gasus* coffins from the Leiden collection is remarkably similar.[180]

5.3.2 Pigments

For centuries of time, the range of pigments available to the ancient craftsmen were either ground-up local or imported minerals, or the manmade Egyptian blue and Egyptian green. The iron-oxide containing earth pigments, which colour can range from a pale yellow to red, purple and dark brown depending on their composition, were the dominating painting material for the red and yellow hues on ancient Egyptian polychrome objects in general. The *Bab el-Gasus* coffin sets in particular show the extensive use of another yellow pigment that was available in this period: orpiment, derived from a sparkly arsenic-sulphide mineral with a bright lemon-yellow colour.

Both pigments have been used for the yellow background colours, either as a single pigment layer, or both pigments mixed in one paint layer, or as separate pigments in a layered stratigraphy where a layer with one pigment was painted on top of the other one. This way, the craftsmen might have manipulated the hue, luminosity

---

177 Technical photography by René Gerritsen, Amsterdam, for the RMO in 2012.
178 B. Kemp, 'Soil (including mud-brick architecture)', in: P.T. Nicholson and I. Shaw (eds), *Ancient Egyptian Materials and Technology*, Cambridge 2000, pp. 78-103, in particular p. 92.

179 Van Walsem, *Djedmonthuiufankh*.
180 Many scholars have observed the colour sequence on coffins, wall paintings et cetera, but to my experience René van Walsem's observations are the most systematic and complete. His excellent understanding of the stratigraphy was developed via observing the surface with just the naked eye, without specialist imaging techniques, paint cross sections or microscopy.

Materials for the polychrome decoration		
0 Support	wood with textile on top	*ficus sycomorus* (identified for lid F 93/10.1a and lid F 93/10.3a)
1 Preparation layers	brown/grey ground	quartz, plant fibers, calcite, wood fibers, biotite, iron-oxides
	white ground	mainly calcite
2 Preliminary sketch	marking-out lines	char black, with use of a straight edge
	under-drawing for text and vignettes	red hematite (mainly iron-oxide)
3 Partially applied preparation layer	bright white layer, in the collar area of lids and mummy boards	magnesium-calcium carbonate (possibly huntite)
4 Paint sequence: yellow	background colour	layer containing yellow orpiment
		or
		layer containing yellow orpiment on top of yellow ochre layer
		or
	partial on inside decoration	layer containing yellow orpiment and yellow ochre mixed
		or
		layer containing yellow orpiment, yellow ochre and calcite mixed
		or
		layer containing yellow orpiment
5 Paint sequence: red	background colour on the inside of coffins	red earth (contains iron-oxide, clays)
		or
	fill of areas in vignettes, outlines	possibly red earth mixed with black on the inside of coffin F 93/10.2a
		or
		red hematite
6 Paint sequence: blue	partial on outside and inside of coffins, partial on coffin lids and mummy boards	Egyptian blue (a manmade calcium-copper-silicate) with bronze remnants as the copper source
7 Paint sequence: green	partially applied	a green copper pigment F 93/10.1a lid
		on the outside of coffin F 93/10.3a: orpiment mixed with Egyptian blue
8 Paint sequence: details	black and white details (eyes and beards of figures)	char black and calcite
9 Coating	overall varnish on outside of coffins, coffin rim, coffin lids and mummy boards (except for F 93/10.3a and F 93/10.4)	*pistacia lentiscus* (mastic resin)
	partial varnish on inside	

Table 3: Overview of the general paint sequence as observed on the four Bab el-Gasus coffins sets in the collection of the RMO, and their identified materials. Analyses by Ulderico Santamaria (Diagnostic Laboratories, Musei Vaticani), Luc Megens and Matthijs de Keijzer (Rijksdienst voor Cultureel Erfgoed, Amsterdam), Jessica Hensel (Restaulab), Casey Mallinckrodt (Virginia Museum of Fine Art), Liliane Mann (independent archaeologist), and Elsbeth Geldhof (Bluetortoise Conservation). Technical imaging by René Gerritsen, Amsterdam.

and opacity of the yellow background colour, making use of the different colour and light reflectance properties of each pigment.[181]

Yellow earths can be sourced almost anywhere and have a long history of use as pigments. However, natural deposits of the mineral orpiment are not that widely geographically available.[182] Although well known as a pigment to ancient societies, it had to be imported into Egypt which resulted in a considerable difference in economic value compared to yellow earths.

A yellow background made with just a yellow earth pigment has been identified on the varnished collar on the mummy board of Tjenetpenherunefer F 93/10.3b, while a complex layered structure, using both pigments, is located on the outer lid and coffin base of Gautseshen F 93/10.1a. None of the *Bab el-Gasus* coffin sets in the collection of the RMO carry a yellow background with solely orpiment, but this has been identified for several 21st Dynasty 'yellow' coffins elsewhere.[183]

5.3.3 Paint Application with Hands or Fingers?

Occasionally finger prints are found in varnish layers, bringing us very near the people who handled the coffins in ancient times. Despite the fact that hands are presumably the most obvious tools for practitioners of any craft, there is very little evidence for the use of hands for the application of paint or the application of preparation layers on coffins or other ancient Egyptian objects. Some archaeologists have found finger strokes in plaster remnants on stone walls[184] and on the basis of *longue durée* polychromy traditions, there is no reason to exclude the application of preparation layers on coffins from this tradition.[185]

Also the stage of applying textile over joints or rough areas in the wood construction, could possibly have been executed with hands as 'work tools'. The textile is glued to the wood with an animal glue,[186] an adhesive that is based on the collagen and related proteins derived from hides, bones or intestines via boiling in water. Gettens and Stout mention a representation of the process of gluing, that includes a brush and glue pot, as well as a piece of dried glue, on a stone carving from Thebes, from the time of Thutmose III.[187] Although this stone carving is depicting a brush, it was learned from own experience that hands were extremely effective for adhering large pieces of textile to a wooden surface using a glue.[188]

5.3.4 Paint Application Using Brushes

Nonetheless is a brush the archetypal painter's tool. Brushes are generally associated with animal hairs, but the majority of the brushes that have been excavated or found as burial goods in the ancient Egyptian context were thought to be made of plant fibers. Reeds from the *Juncus Maritimus*,[189] or date palm fibers[190] have been mostly identified. Also plant fibers that were processed into rope first, could be re-used for making brushes by tying the rope together and fraying out the ends, an example of which is in the collection of the British Museum.[191]

---

181 H. Strudwick, M. Strong, and E. Geldhof, 'Seeing Coffins in a New Light: Materiality and Perception.' Paper presented at *Bab el-Gasus in Context. Egyptian Funerary Culture During the 21st Dynasty*. The Gate of the Priests Bab el-Gasus Project, Lisbon 19-20 September 2016.

182 R.D. Harley, *Artists' Pigments c. 1600-1835. A Study in English Documentary Sources* (second revised edition), London 1982, pp. 89 and 93.

183 For example, the outer coffin, inner coffin and mummy board of the coffin set of Nespawershefyt, which are similar 'yellow coffins', all have a wash of orpiment on top of the white preparation layer. H. Strudwick and J. Dawson, Catalogue entry '26: Coffin set of Nespawershefyt', in: J. Dawson et al, 'Egyptian Coffins: Materials, Construction and Decoration', in: *Death on the Nile. Uncovering the Afterlife of Ancient Egypt*, London 2016, pp. 182-189.

184 J. Toivari-Viitala, 'Workmen's huts in the Theban Mountains'. Presentation for the Netherlands Institute for the Near East, Leiden, 12 December 2013. The archaeologists observed fingerprints as well as wooden spatula marks on remnants of plaster on limestone wall fragments.

185 The paint layering and painting technique on 21st Dynasty coffins are comparable to those on Italian panel paintings – for which the painters handbook of Cennino Cennini is one of the earliest manuscript to document this. Cennini also describes the application of gesso layers with the hands, on stone sculpture, *cf.* C. d'Andrea Cennini, *The Craftsman's Handbook "Il Libro dell'Arte"* Translated by Daniel V. Thompson Jr, New York 1933, Dover edition 1954, pp. 118-119: "How to gild a stone figure. (…) Then take gesso sottile or gilders' gesso, (…) and begin by putting the first coat of it on the job, rubbing it down with your hand very perfectly."
De Diversis Artibus by Theophilus Presbyter, a much earlier treatise from circa 1125, mentions only a brush for laying on gesso on hide and wood (it does not mention stone sculpture) Book 1 section XIX. *Cf.* C.R. Dodwell, *Theophilus. The Various Arts. De Diversis Artibus. Edited and translated by C.R. Dodwell.* Oxford Medieval Texts, Oxford 1961.

186 Material analysis by Ulderico Santamaria, head of the Diagnostic Laboratories of the Vatican Museums, for the RMO in 2012.

187 R.J. Gettens and G.L. Stout. *Painting Materials. A Short Encyclopaedia.* (1942), unabridged and corrected republication New York 1966, p. 27.

188 Author's experience with reconstructing part of the inner lid of the 21st Dynasty coffin set of Nespawershefyt, for the Fitzwilliam Museum, University of Cambridge, in 2016.

189 R. Drenkhahn, 'Pinsel', in: W. Helck (ed.), *Lexikon der Ägyptologie* IV, Wiesbaden 1982, pp. 1053-1054.

190 For example: Petrie Museum UC 27991.

191 British Museum EA 36893 and EA 36889.

Figure 26 (left): Black marking-out lines for positioning the text bands, confidently drawn with a hollow pen along a straight edge, on the outer lid of Nestanebtawy F 93/10.2a. Photo: Elsbeth Geldhof.

Figure 27 (right): Glaze of Egyptian Blue on top of a bright white (possibly huntite) layer. Detail from the collar on the outer lid of Gautseshen F 93/10.1a. The huntite layer is no longer recognisable as a white layer because of the yellowed varnish on top. Light that is transmitted through the varnish and blue glaze, is still reflected on the bright magnesium-calcium carbonate layer underneath. Photo: Elsbeth Geldhof.

Broad brushstrokes in the ground layers are visible on many of the coffins, indicating that the white under-layers have not been burnished before applying the coloured decoration. The brush strokes are about 5 cm wide and follow scattered half circular patterns, just like anybody today would apply a paint coat. The brushstrokes are visible because of the use of relatively coarse pigments and a water-based binding medium (mainly gum arabic). A paint with this combination of materials is not able to form a smooth film with drying, and therefore the brush strokes remain visible.

Finer brushes have been used for the red, blue and green sections of the polychromy. Hollow pens were also used: characteristic marks of pens, executed along a straight edge, are visible on the marking-out lines that divide the coffin surface into the areas for text, and for decorative scenes. These lines are there to help the painter and are not meant to be seen in the final product. However, many coffins, lids and mummy boards do reveal some of this pen-work either because it has not been removed or because the under-drawing lines extend the initial intention. Extremely well executed pen-work is visible on the outer coffin lid and base of the coffin set of Nesytanebtawy F 93/10.2a (Fig. 26).

5.3.5 Underdrawing Techniques

On the coffins underdrawings can be distinguished, either in black or red. On the Leiden coffins, black underdrawing lines are often applied specifically to mark the text bands, either on top or underneath the yellow background layer. The elaborate process for drawing the black lines is visible on Gautseshen's outer coffin (F 93/10.1a). There, the width of the text bands was first marked with charcoal before drawn with black paint, using a reed pen along a straight edge. Later in the paint sequence, these black underdrawings were then painted over in Egyptian blue. A similar process for creating underdrawings for text bands can be found on the outer coffin and lid of Nesytanebtawy (F 93/10.2a).

The black lines can be seen with the naked eye where the Egyptian blue paint has not covered the lines. On this same outer coffin, *pentimenti*[192] are visible: the vertical text bands were initially intended higher in the black underdrawing stage and this has been changed in the final paintwork. These black lines for marking the text bands

---

192 '*Pentimenti*' are alterations in the composition of a painting, evidenced by traces of earlier work that are painted over, and are indications that the artist or craftsman has changed his mind.

Figure 28: Paint cross section in regular light (left section) and UV radiance (right section) showing the layering of the yellow colour on the lid of Nesytanebtawy F 93/10.2a: a layer of orpiment on top of a layer of yellow ochre. Photo: Ulderico Santamaria, Musei Vaticani.

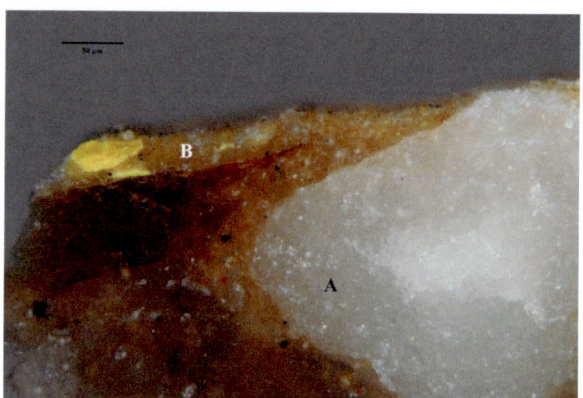

Figure 30: Paint cross section in regular light showing the layering of the yellow colour on the lid of the inner coffin of Tjenetpenherunefer F 93/10.3a: orpiment and yellow ochre mixed with calcite. Photo: Ulderico Santamaria, Musei Vaticani.

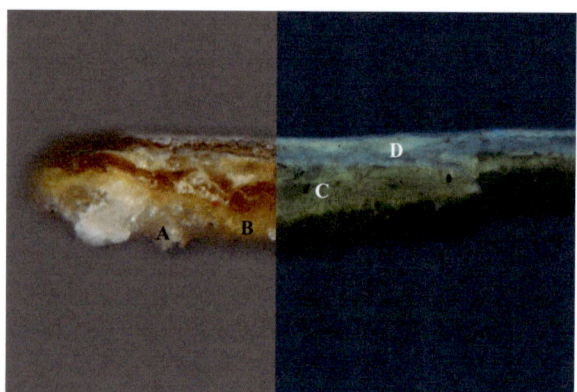

Figure 29: Paint cross section in regular light (left) and UV radiance (right) showing the layering of the yellow colour on the lid of an anonymous man in the coffin set of Nesytanebtawy F 93/10.2a: yellow ochre and orpiment mixed in one layer. Photo: Ulderico Santamaria, Musei Vaticani.

Figure 31: Coarse particles of orpiment pigment, visible with the naked eye, were purposely added to the varnish on the outer lid of Nesytanebtawy F 93/10.2a. Photo: Elsbeth Geldhof.

are particularly well visible on the false colour Infrared images[193] that were generated by Fabio Morresi, conservation scientist at the *Musei Vaticani*.

The position and shape of large areas (such as the semi-circular shape of the collars on the lids) have been marked out in red, directly on the white preparation layer. Understandably these underdrawings were not meant to be visible in the final product. In many cases, technical imaging using infrared can visualise underdrawings when they are done in black and when they are not too far down in the stratigraphy. Because of their red colour, these red underdrawings are only visible in locations where they are uncovered because of paint losses.

5.3.6 The Use of White for a Three-dimensional Effect

Several lids and mummy boards have semi-circular collars where flowers, leafs and berries are painted as if they are draped in garlands over the chest. The leafs and berries are very stylised, but have some three-dimensionality to them because of the use of outlines, colour contrasts and glazes (Fig. 27). These collar areas also have an extra white layer within their stratigraphy, that is applied on top of the general white calcite preparation layer.[194] This second white layer is much brighter than the regular white preparation layer because of the use of a more unusual magnesium-calcium-carbonate pigment (possibly huntite). The orpiment and Egyptian blue glazes, and often the addition of varnish in the collar areas, seems to be directly related to this bright white layer: the glazes are light-transmitting and allow the light to be reflected on this bright white layer, thus contributing to the lifelike effect of the painted fruit and flower garlands. This painting technique can be found at all the collar areas on the Leiden coffin lids and mummy boards, with the exception of the lid of the inner coffin of Tjenetpenherunefer (F 93/10.3a).

5.3.7 The Yellow Background Colour

The characteristic yellow background colour of these coffins and mummy boards, are probably the result of a careful chosen paint methodology that took into account the hue, luminosity, opacity of the two available yellow pigments (yellow earth and orpiment), as well as the cost effectiveness of these two pigments.

The yellow earths with their fine, granular texture and orangey-yellow colour are very different from the costly orpiment, that has a much higher light reflectance because of its crystal structure and has, in general, a bright lemon-yellow colour. Craftsmen could also add the cheap, and opaque white calcite which would have an impact on the final yellow hue as well. Mixing the two yellows, layering one on top of the other, or mixing in calcite, are therefore great opportunities for painters to manipulate the economics as well as the optical properties of the yellow background colour.

In fact, all varieties of mixtures and layering were observed on the Leiden coffin sets. The yellow background colour on the lid of Nesytanebtawy (F 93/10.2a) consists of a layer of orpiment on top of a layer with yellow earth. The inner coffin of an anonymous man (F 93/10.2b), part of the same coffin set, shows a mixture of yellow earth and orpiment. The pale background colour on the inner coffin of Tjenepenherunefer (F 93/10.3a) has calcite mixed in the yellow earth-orpiment mixture.

Superimposed layers of paint, and pigment mixtures within paint layers cannot be investigated from the surface of a coffin. The stratigraphy can be investigated and identified via paint cross sections and pigment analysis of every paint layer. A paint cross section gives a transverse view of the paint layering under high magnification varying from 100x to 500x. Individual pigment particles can then be identified using specialist techniques such as SEM/EDX[195] which identifies chemical elements in individual particles. An overview of the yellow background layers can be found in the table below, and figures 28-30 are examples of paint cross sections that show the varieties of layering and mixing of pigments.

5.3.8 Sgraffito

Although not strictly a paint application technique, *sgraffito* is a decoration technique that is based on superimposing two different coloured layers and then scraping away the top layer in a pattern to reveal the layer underneath.[196] This technique has been applied on for example the mummy board of Nesytanebtawy (F 93/10.2c). The yellow of the lines in the green and red border in the collar of this mummy board is in fact the yellow orpiment overall background layer showing through (Fig. 32). This technique may also have been used for the inside decora-

---

193 False colour Infrared imaging makes use of differences in reflectance of pigments, in the Infrared wavelengths. As the infrared wavelengths are outside of the visible spectrum, false colour infrared images can capture characteristics of a painted surface that are invisible to the human eye.

194 Analysis by Ulderico Santamaria (Diagnostic Laboratories of the Vatican Museums) for the RMO in 2012.

195 Scanning electron microscopy-energy-dispersive X-ray Spectroscopy (SEM/EDX) is a is a method for elemental analysis of paint samples. This technique can help identifying inorganic pigments by locating heavy elements within a layered structure, when used on a paint cross section. For example, the detection of Fe (iron) within a yellow coloured particle can lead to the identification of a yellow earth, that mainly consists of iron-oxide.

196 G. Vasari, *Vasari On Technique. Being the Introduction to The Three Arts of Design, Architecture, Sculpture, and Painting, Prefixed to the Lives of the Most Excellent Painters, Sculptors and Architects* (translated into English by Louisa S. Maclehose), London 1907, p. 243.

Figure 32 (left): A sgraffito technique has been used to create the yellow lines in the green and red border in the collar area of the mummy board of an anonymous man in the coffin set of Nesytanebtawy F 93/10.2c. Photo: Elsbeth Geldhof.

Figure 33 (right): The many stars on the dark blue background on the inside decoration of the outer coffin of Gautseshen F 93/10.1a, are possibly also created using the sgraffito technique Photo: Elsbeth Geldhof.

Leiden inventory number	Composition of yellow colour
F 93/10.1a box and lid	- magnesium-calcium carbonate layer under collar decoration - orpiment layer on top of yellow ochre layer
F 93/10.1b box and lid	- magnesium-calcium carbonate layer under collar decoration - orpiment layer on top of yellow ochre layer
F 93/10.1c mummy board	- magnesium-calcium carbonate layer under collar decoration - orpiment layer on top of yellow ochre layer
F 93/10.2a box and lid	- orpiment on top of yellow ochre - lid: also orpiment and yellow ochre mixed (redecoration)
F 93/10.2b box and lid	orpiment and yellow ochre mixed
F 93/10.2c mummy board	magnesium-calcium carbonate (possibly huntite) layer under collar decoration
F 93/10.3a box and lid	orpiment, yellow ochre and calcite mixed
F 93/10.3b mummy board	yellow ochre mixed with calcite and quartz
F 93/10.4 box and lid	No data on mixtures or layering was collected for this coffin, although pXRF* spectra confirms As (arsenic) in yellow background and Fe (iron) as the highest reflected element, indicating the use of both orpiment and yellow earth.

Table 4: Overview of the composition and stratigraphy of the yellow background colours of the Leiden Bab el-Gasus coffin sets. Analyses by Ulderico Santamaria (Diagnostic Laboratories, Musei Vaticani), Luc Megens and Matthijs de Keijzer (Rijksdienst voor Cultureel Erfgoed, Amsterdam), Jessica Hensel (Restaulab), Casey Mallinckrodt (Virginia Museum of Fine Art), Liliane Mann, and Elsbeth Geldhof (Bluetortoise Conservation).

* Portable X-ray Fluorescence spectrometry (pXRF) is a method for locating heavy elements on a painted surface, using a portable device. This is a quick and non-invasive method that helps with starting to identify inorganic pigments.

Figure 34: The low relief in pastiglia technique, here on the outer lid of Gautseshen F 93/10.1a. Photo: Jonathan Gration.

tion of the outer and inner coffins of Gautseshen (F 93/10.1a, -b) and Nesytanebtawy (F 93/10.2a, -b). The stars in the dark blue bands seem to be created by scratching away the blue to reveal the white from the layer underneath (Fig. 33).

5.3.9 Pastiglia

Pastiglia is a low relief decoration technique in a white paste, which can be gilded, painted or left plain.[197] This technique can be found on polychrome sculpture, panel paintings, furniture and decorative objects from the Late Middle Ages and Renaissance onwards, but has also been identified on ancient Egyptian objects.[198] On the coffin lids, a *pastiglia* technique has been used for making the scarabs, sun disks and deities in low relief (Fig. 34). The *pastiglia* has been applied during the white preparation stage and this suggests that from very early on in the decoration process, it was decided which elements would be executed in low relief. Any changes in the design afterwards would require taking away or changing the *pastiglia* elements, which might be the reason for continuing large parts of the decoration when adapting the coffin for a new owner.[199]

Generally, there are several methods for creating a low relief in *pastiglia*. The white paste that is used for the preparation layers can also be applied to form an organic, round shape with a low relief. This particular technique has been used on the Leiden coffin sets.

---

197 M.S. Frinta, 'Raised Gilded Adornment of the Cypriot Icons and the Occurrence of the Technique in the West', *Gesta* XX No. 2 (1981), pp. 333-347.

198 H. Kühn *et al.*, *Reclams Handbuch der künstlerischen Techniken. Band 1: Farbmittel, Buchmalerei, Tafel- und Leinwandmalerei*, Ditzingen 1997, p. 170.

199 For example, only the face and wig of the outer lid of Nesytanebtawy (F 93/10.2a) seem to have been adapted for the second owner, leaving large parts of the decoration, including those done in the *pastiglia* technique, unchanged.

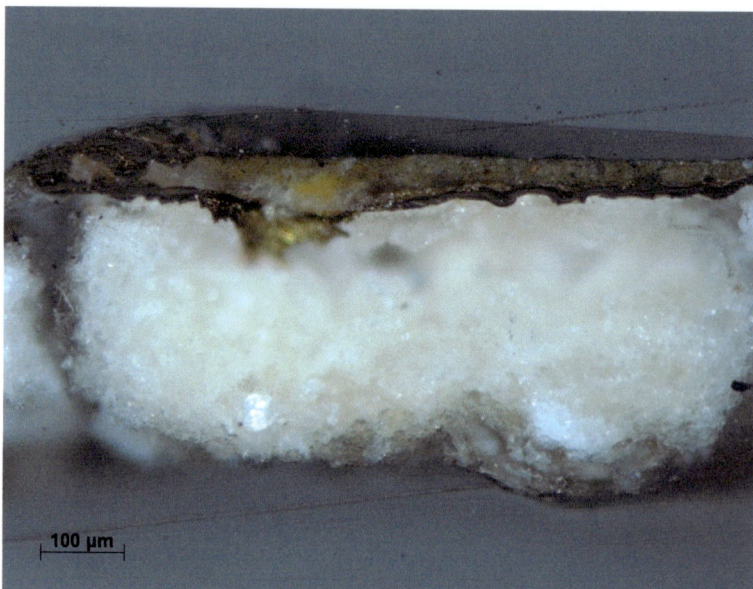

A second method involved making the organic round shapes crisper by edging off the sides, for example with a wooden stick, a flint knife or a piece of metal. This technique is known to have been used on mummy coffins from this period and later, and may have been used on the lid of the inner coffin of an anonymous man (F 93/10.4).

The white paste can also be pre-formed in a mould, and then attached to the surface. This technique is very common on western panel paintings and polychrome sculpture of the Middle Ages and Renaissance, but has yet to be identified on ancient Egyptian artefacts.

5.3.10 Gold

The complete coffin set of Gautseshen (F 93/10.1a, -b, -c), now with their heads absent, would have originally had gilded faces. This can be read from the remnants of gold in the neck of the lids and the mummy board, that appeared after removal of filling material that was added at later restorations (Fig. 35). The gold has been applied as a foil: the thickness is about 20 micron (Fig. 36),[200] much more substantial than what we know as gold leaf in the western world from the Renaissance onwards.

According to Spike Bucklow's study,[201] the current high priced status of gold can be completely attributed to the traditional world, as by the Middle Ages the European sources of gold were exhausted forcing the craftsmen of the modern world to hoard, loot, trade and re-cycle the existing sources of gold. By that time, very little of the gold was derived from European sources, the majority originating in Arabia, India, or Egypt, from natural sources as well as from golden objects that might have been in circulation since Antiquity.[202] In fact, the looting or robbing of ancient Egyptian tombs from their valuables has been a well-known threat for millennia. Therefore it may come as no surprise that, at the arrival of the *Bab el-Gasus* coffin sets in Leiden in 1893, it was noted that the missing faces on the coffin set of the Gautseshen must have been stolen by tomb-robbers.

Figure 35 (right): Gold remnant in neck area of the lid of F 93/10.1a. Photo: Elsbeth Geldhof.

Figure 36 (left): Section of the neck, showing the gold foil on the lid of outer coffin F 93/10.1a and paint cross section in regular light. Photo: Luc Megens, Rijksdienst Cultureel Erfgoed.

---

200 Analysis by Luc Megens (*Rijksdienst voor Cultureel Erfgoed*) for the RMO in 2011.
201 S. Bucklow, *The Alchemy of Paint. Art, Science and Secrets from the Middle Ages,* London 2009.
202 Bucklow, *Alchemy of Paint*, pp. 173-176 and J. Ogden 'Metals', in: P.T. Nicholson and I. Shaw (eds), *Ancient Egyptian Materials and Technology*, Cambridge 2000, pp. 148-176, in particular pp. 161-164.

The gold foil is applied on a homogenous white paste layer with an unknown and undetectable mordant (which is the 'glue' to affix gold leaf to a surface).[203]

In general, the use of gold leaf or gold foil and their mordants on objects from the ancient world has not been subject to material analysis very often. Sandrine Pagès-Camagna has identified gold foil applied to a red or yellow paint layer, and has identified gum arabic as a mordant.[204] A similar layering was identified by Ioanna Kakkouli in her study of ancient Greek wall paintings: in two cases, foil of electrum (a natural alloy of gold and silver) was applied on a yellow intermediate layer with gum Arabic as the mordant.[205]

5.3.11 Varnish

Many objects have been varnished with a mastic resin, that can turn brown-yellow with natural ageing. An aged varnish has a huge impact on the present readability of the surface, which might have been a reason for removing varnishes from coffins in the past. The lid of the inner coffin of an anonymous man (F 93/10.2b) has been restored between 1972-1976[206] and the 'before' photos show a heavily darkened, opaque varnish layer (Fig. 37). According to the restoration report, this was at the time recognised as the original varnish and was removed mechanically for aesthetic reasons. After removal, a modern, synthetic varnish was applied. This procedure was possibly a decision that did not arouse much discussion. At the time, removal and re-application of varnishes was common practice in the tradition of other varnished museum objects, such as old master easel painting or medieval polychrome sculpture, where the varnish is considered a technical layer meant to saturate the painted surface.

As a result of study over the course of several decades, researchers and scientists of ancient Egyptian polychrome objects are now concluding that the varnish should be considered part of the paint stratigraphy and contributes to the material integrity of the archaeological object.[207] Some scholars also suspect religious reasons for varnishing coffins, mainly because of the use of mastic resin as a fragrant in temple rituals. There were in fact many varieties of mastic resin available to the ancient Egyptian society, both from local sources and abroad. Whether or not these varieties were sourced, and used for specific purposes only, is not yet understood.[208]

Mastic resin is a sticky, water-resistant substance from the *Pistacia* tree. A large amount of mastic resins on ancient Egyptian objects that could be identified, seem to be sourced from the *Pistacia Lentiscus*.[209] The Greek island of Chios was the main supplier of mastic resin in the ancient world, although it can also be found in nowadays Portugal, Morocco, and the Canary Islands.[210] The mastic resin appears as translucent, pale yellow, malleable drops, which have to be modified for use as a brushable varnish. This could be established by heating the resin drops, with or without the addition of a solvent (an

---

203 Analysis by Matthijs de Keijzer (*Rijksdienst voor Cultureel Erfgoed*), for the RMO in 2012.
204 S. Pagès-Camagna, 'Les matériaux au peintre: du contour au remplissage', in: G. Andreu-Lanoë et al. (eds) *L'art du Contour: Le dessin dans l'Egypte ancienne*, Paris 2013.
205 I. Kakoulli, *Greek Painting Techniques and Materials from the fourth to the First Century BC.*, London 2009, p. 60.
206 '*Restauratieverslag van een deksel van een sarcofaag in het bezit van het Rijksmuseum voor Oudheden in Leiden*' archived at the *Rijksdienst voor Cultureel Erfgoed* (RCE) under object number 716 document number 71/17.
207 D.A. Scott 'A review of ancient Egyptian pigments and cosmetics', *Studies in Conservation* 61 (July 2016) pp. 185-202.
208 M. Serpico, with a contribution by R. White, 'Resins, amber and bitumen', in: P.T. Nicholson and I. Shaw (eds), *Ancient Egyptian Materials and Technology*, Cambridge 2000, pp. 430-474, in particular pp. 434-436.
209 R. Stacey, 'Paint media and varnishes', in: A. Middleton and K. Uprichard (eds), *The Nebamun Wall Paintings. Conservation, Scientific Analysis and Display at the British Museum*, London 2008, pp. 51-60; and analysis by Ulderico Santamaria, head of the Diagnostic laboratories of the Vatican Museums, for the RMO in 2012.
210 Gettens and Stout, *Painting Materials*, p. 34.

Figure 37: The lid of the inner coffin of an anonymous man, in the set of Nesytanebtawy (F 93/10.2b), has been restored in 1972-1976 at the then Centraal Laboratorium in Amsterdam. This photo of the lid, made before treatment, show how ancient varnishes can change to heavily darkened, brittle and opaque coatings, due to natural ageing processes over millennia of time. Photo: anonymous photographer, Rijksdienst voor het Cultureel Erfgoed (RCE) archived under object number 716, document number 71/17.

oil or a spirit) that would have increased the workability of the varnish.[211] However, the detection of a solvent or oil addition to the varnish seems to be difficult despite increasingly sophisticated analysis techniques. Serpico and White have found proof of heating, on samples of three varnished objects in the collection of the British Museum.[212]

---

211 Gettens and Stout, *Painting Materials*, p. 57: "The solvent power of turpentine was known as early as 460 BCE and was referred to by Pliny." However, the earliest record of mastic as a spirited varnish dates from 16th century Italy. The earliest record of mastic as an oil varnish is from the 9th century. See also: A.P. Laurie, *Materials of the Painter's Craft in Europe and Egypt From Earliest Times to the End of the XVIIIth Century, With Some Account of their Preparation and Use,* London 1910, p. 287.

212 M. Serpico and R. White, 'The Use and Identification of Varnish on New Kingdom Funerary Equipment', in: W.V. Davies (ed.), *Colour and Painting in Ancient Egypt,* London 2001, pp. 33-42.

Coffin element	Pigmented varnish	Analytical method
F 93/10.1a (outer coffin Gautseshen)	orpiment in the mastic varnish on outer coffin and lid	cross section microscopy, SEM-EDX
F 93/10.2a (outer coffin Nesytanebtawy)	extremely coarse orpiment in the mastic varnish on outer coffin and lid	cross section microscopy, SEM-EDX
F 93/10.2b (inner coffin of anonymous man, in coffin set of Nesytanebtawy)	orpiment, Egyptian Blue, and yellow ochre in varnish, possibly pigments ended up in the varnish because of picking up from layers below the varnish (non-intentional pigmented varnish)	cross section microscopy, SEM-EDX
F 93/10.2c (mummy board of anonymous man, in coffin set of Nesytanebtawy)	orpiment in mastic varnish on mummy board	cross section microscopy, SEM-EDX
F 93/10.3b (mummy board of Tjenetpenherunefer)	yellow ochre in mastic varnish on text band	cross section microscopy, SEM-EDX

Table 5: Overview of the varnished coffin elements of the Leiden Bab el-Gasus sets, that carry a pigment in their varnish. Analysis by Ulderico Santamaria (Diagnostic Laboratories of the Musei Vaticani) for the RMO in 2012.

Mastic resin drops are of a pale colour with a certain translucency. By heating, the natural ageing process is accelerated and the resin will turn brown-yellow. A resin dissolved in an oil or spirit however, will start with a pale colour. The modification method of the mastic resin drops for making a varnish, is therefore an important factor in the discussion about the intentional colour characteristics and meaning of a varnish application in ancient times, in particular in the context of 21st Dynasty 'yellow' coffins.

Several of the Leiden *Bab el-Gasus* coffins carry a pigment in their varnish. Pigments might unintentionally end up in the sticky, slow drying varnish, but for some of the Leiden coffins, a yellow orpiment pigment seems to have been purposely added to the varnish. The main basis for this thought is the fact that the yellow orpiment particles in the varnish are much coarser than the yellow orpiment particles in the yellow background layer.[213] Coarse orpiment particles in the varnish layer are instantly visible, with the naked eye, on the lid of the outer coffin of Nesytanebtawy F 93/10.2a (Fig. 31).

5.4 Workshop Methodologies

Workshop methodologies can be investigated by focusing on a certain painting technique or design feature on several coffins and mummy boards. Some coffins of the Leiden sets show similar semi-circular shapes above figures in the vignettes, which refer to a baldachin giving shelter to figures beneath. In this particular example, the painting direction for these semi-circular shapes give away the 'hand of the painter': a brush stroke starting on the right side would have been drawn by a left-handed painter, and vice versa. The baldachins on both coffins of Gautseshen (F 93/10.1a, -b) and the outer coffin of Nesytanebtawy (F 93/10.2a) have a very similar rendering, but those on Gautseshen's coffins are painted by a left-handed painter while those on Nesytanebtawy's outer coffin were painted by a right-handed person. The inner coffin of Tjenetpenherunefer (F 93/10.3a) however, has very similar baldachins, but painted with two brush strokes going left and right, starting at the top. Therefore there is no specific information about the dominant hand of this particular painter (Fig. 38).

Comparing the rendering of a specific iconographic element over a series of coffins, can give an insight in what painting techniques one could use for creating something similar. The outer and inner coffins of Gautseshen (F 93.10/1a, -b), the outer coffin of Nesytanebtawy (F 93/10.2a) and the inner coffin of Tjenetpenherunefer (F 93/10.3a) all have a similar rendering of the Hathor cow descending the West mountain. This scene is almost identical on the coffins of Gautseshen and Tjenetpenherunefer; the only real difference is the amount of filling in of elements in the blue and the green stages of the painting process. The outer coffin of Nesytanebtawy (F 93/10.2a) pictures a reclined

---

213 Analysis by Ulderico Santamaria (Diagnostic Laboratories of the *Musei Vaticani*) for the RMO in 2012.

Figure 38: A left handed painter on the outer coffin of Gautseshen F 93/10.1a and a right-handed painter on the outer coffin of Nesytanebtawy F 93/10.2a. Photo: Elsbeth Geldhof.

Figure 39: Comparison of the rendering of the spots on the Hathor cows depicted on the outer and inner coffins of Gautseshen F 93/10.1a, -b; the outer coffin of Nesytanebtawy F 93/10.2a and the inner coffin of Tjenetpenherunefer F 93/10.3a.

cow instead of a walking one. The study of the painting techniques for these Hathor cows focused on the spots on the cows' bodies. We then turned to experimental archaeology to find out more about the painting tools that were used for creating the spots. For this purpose, reconstructions of ancient Egyptian brushes were made from rope, plant fibers and bundled sticks.[214] The marks from these reconstructed brushes were then compared with the spots on these four Hathor cows. One conclusion was that the spots on the three walking Hathor cows had all been done with a brush that was a bundle of fine sticks, but with a different 'handwriting' on the inner coffin of Tjenetpenherunefer from the coffins of Gautseshen. The spots on the reclining Hathor cow on the outer coffin of Nesytanebtawy were done with a different brush, which was made from rope, or fine plant fibers (Fig. 39).

The investigation of the workflow on a coffin base, lid or mummy board can also help in understanding workshop methodology. Due to the density of decoration elements (*horror vacui*) the painting must have required a lot of concentration, in particular because the painters worked with just one colour at a time. Presumably, painters would have had to keep track of where they were in the decoration process. A work disruption, work that had to be carried over to the next day, an absent co-worker, time pressure from supervisors – basically any situation that would have caused a loss of concentration, would show in the final execution of the design. Omissions can be observed on all coffins of the Leiden *Bab el-Gasus* sets, in the red and blue stage as well as the final green stage. As an example, the outer coffin of Gautseshen (F 93/10.1a) and the inner coffin of the set of Nesytanebtawy (F 93/10.2b) both show relatively many locations where the rendering with a certain colour has been forgotten.

5.5 Conclusion

Despite their often bright and colourful appearance, the pigments, binding mediums, varnish layers and wooden structure of ancient Egyptian mummy coffins are far from a static and stable entity. Over time, deterioration processes that are inherent to the originally used materials can significantly change the appearance of a polychrome surface. To help us with a better understanding of the materiality of polychrome ancient Egyptian objects, a variety of material analyses is nowadays more or less a standard procedure of any preliminary research prior to conservation. Following the Vatican Coffin Project Analysis Protocol, an investigation of the painting techniques, painting tools and paint application has been included in the preliminary research of the four *Bab el-Gasus* coffins sets in Leiden, mainly because of their complex paint stratigraphy and extensive restoration history.

This preliminary research was carried out primarily to prepare for conservation treatment. However, scientific material analysis and a focused investigation of the painting techniques can also bring us very near the ancient craftsmen, their individual characteristics and their daily practice.

In the light of their generic classification of 'yellow coffins', the many ways the painter could influence their yellow appearance has been researched: from using different yellow pigments for the background colour, to manipulating the colour of the varnish by adding pigment or heating of the varnish resin. By investigating the paint application methods, the skilful use of tools to set out a design or to establish a low or high relief via *sgraffito* and *pastiglia*, has come to light.

The knowledge and understanding of the painting techniques is therefore extremely valuable for carefully 'managing the process of change' within the coffins – which is how, in general, 'conservation' might be defined.

The investigation of painting techniques relies on material analysis and technical imaging, and is at present limited to the research of single objects. However, the collaborative efforts in context of the Vatican Coffin Project have the ability to expand this research beyond the particulars of individual coffins, and contribute to a better general understanding of individual craftsmen's skills, coffin decoration techniques and workshop methodology.

---

214 The ancient Egyptian brushes in the collection of the British Museum served as an example: BM EA 36893 and BM EA 36889.

Chapter 6

Coffin Reuse in the 21st Dynasty: A Case Study of the Coffins in the *Rijksmuseum van Oudheden*[215]

Kathlyn M. Cooney

6.1 Introduction

In this contribution, I will lay out detailed evidence for reuse of coffins in the *Rijksmuseum van Oudheden* dating to 21st and early 22nd Dynasties, when the whole of the Mediterranean region went through a massive economic and social collapse, seeing the fall of the Mycenaean, Hittite, Ugaritic, and other civilizations. This regional event didn't bring about Egypt's fall, but it did bring with it disruptions in Egypt's centralised government, economic systems, agriculture, trade networks, not to mention an influx of Sea Peoples and Libyans in mass migrations. Government systems in the north of Egypt faltered, while in Thebes people moved on without a king, relying only on a decentralised High Priesthood of Amun to maintain order.[216]

Coffins are social documents, recording social place, gender, spending ability, geographic place, commodity availability, craft details, and religious information. Coffins can reflect human reactions to all sorts of changes in the environment and within human systems, including reactions to scarcity and crisis. In fact, using coffins to gauge the severity of a social crisis might be a better indicator than official texts with a state agenda of cracking down on opportunists or presenting an image of control. During the New Kingdom and Third Intermediate Period, Egyptians with disposable income were meant to have a nesting coffin set for their death, for their display in the funeral cortège, transformation in burial rites, and, ostensibly, for their use in the hereafter in perpetuity. When the ancient Egyptians entered a period of scarcity and collapse, they were loath to abandon the physicality of their coffins, and Theban elites in particular continued their

---

215 There are many people I need to thank for facilitating my research in Leiden, not least among them Christian Greco, who was curator there when I started my reuse research, and Elsbeth Geldhof, once a conservator with duties at the *Rijksmuseum van Oudheden* and now my chief partner-in-crime when investigating coffins for reuse, and, more importantly, proving the reuse with all of her many tools. I would also like to thank Maarten Raven, curator, for all his generosity and help, as well as René van Walsem and Rob Demarée who both stopped by storage from time to time to visit the work. Remy Hiramoto facilitated the photography, both infrared and conventional, and I could not have done the work without him.

216 N. Reeves, *Valley of the Kings. The Decline of a Royal Necropolis*, London 1990. See also J.H. Taylor, 'Aspects of the History of the Valley of the Kings in the Third Intermediate Period', in: N. Reeves (ed.), *After Tut`Ankhamun. Research and Excavation in the Royal Necropolis at Thebes*, London 1992.

materialist understanding of funerary practices creating coffins with brightly painted polychrome decorations. How did the Egyptians maintain coffin production despite scarcity of resources, known to us from other texts and sources?

When I first started my dissertation in 1999, I set out to find all examples of Ramesside coffins in museums in Europe, North America, and Egypt. There were only about 80 examples, including small fragments,[217] and this, despite the fact that the first part of the Ramesside Period was characterised by prosperity, including empire building, the astounding building program of Ramesses II, the apex of the Deir el-Medina craft production in the Valley of the Kings, and intensive funerary commissions by elites in Western Thebes. Despite the evidence for significant elite funerary production from the reigns of Ramesses I to Ramesses III, very few coffins can be attributed to the 19th Dynasty and even fewer to the 20th Dynasty. Where have all the Ramesside coffins gone? It was Andrzej Niwiński who first suggested that many such coffins were actually reused in the ensuing 21st Dynasty[218] when social and governmental systems decentralised and when evidence for economic scarcity is everywhere in the written and archaeological record, but there was no systematic study of the issue.

Identifying reuse on later coffins of the 21st Dynasty can be very difficult. Unless one is specifically looking for it, it can hide in plain sight, partly because we consider coffin reuse aberrant and do not expect to see it, but also because the Egyptians became very skilled at creating new coffins out of old.

Mine is the first study to systematically identify evidence of coffin reuse in any time period in ancient Egypt. Because we are moving from a phase of prosperity to one of scarcity in the 21st Dynasty, the study of coffin reuse must view trends as they change over time and employ a large dataset. The larger the dataset, the more reliable the study's conclusions about trends of reuse will be. Thus, I set out with an interdisciplinary team of experts to examine as many coffins of the 19th-21st Dynasties and early 22nd Dynasty as possible, looking under breaks in the plaster for older decoration, examining the spots where personal names were written for evidence of re-inscription, carefully checking for out-of-fashion wooden modelled feet or forearms underneath the current plaster surface.

There are many ways to reuse a coffin. Sometimes, only the old name is removed and a new one added. Many other coffins indicate that craftsmen updated funerary pieces in a piecemeal fashion, keeping some elements and re-working others – keeping an older style wig, for example, covering it over with blue paint only, but updating the collar and lower body. Or, in other cases, I have been able to identify forearms and elbows as older 19th Dynasty coffin modelling that was retained and then covered over with later 21st Dynasty design. Other coffins showed signs of having been changed from female type (with earrings, flat hands, and breasts) to masculine type (with a striped headdress, fisted hands, and a beard). Other coffins show that they were scraped down of all old decoration before new plaster and paint are applied; I can only see this technique if the craft specialists left remnants of the old decoration.

Thus far, I have found only one 19th Dynasty coffin that might possibly have been reused (the inner coffin of Katebet in the British Museum[219]); it shows a change in gender, from a male wig to a female. No other signs of modification are visible on the

---

217 Cooney, *Cost of Death*. This research focused mainly on Theban coffins, and I have added many more 19th and 20th Dynasty coffins to the growing list, which will appear in K.M. Cooney, 'The End of New Kingdom Egypt: How Ancient Egyptian Funerary Materials Can Help Us Understand Society in Crisis', in: U. Rummel and S. Kubisch (eds), *The Ramesside Period in Egypt: Studies into Cultural and Historical Processes of the 19th and 20th Dynasties, Proceedings of the International Symposium Held at Heidelberg, 5th to 7th June, 2015*, Wiesbaden, forthcoming) and K.M. Cooney, 'Ramesside Body Containers of Wood and Cartonnage from Northern Egyptian Necropolises', in: V. Verschoor *et al.* (eds), *Festschrift for René Van Walsem*, Leiden (forthcoming).
218 Niwiński, *21st Dynasty Coffins*, p. 57.
219 BM EA 6665, cf. e.g. W.R. Dawson and P.H.K. Gary, *Catalogue of Egyptian Antiquities in the British Museum: Mummies and Human Remains* 1, London 1968, pp. 52 and 145.

Rate of reuse for 20th-22nd Dynasty coffins analysed thus far								
Museum/Institution	Coffins	0	0.5-1	2	3	TBD	Excluded	Reuse %
Berlin, Germany, *Ägyptisches Museum*	23	11	4	1	4	1	2	39.13%
Bodrhyddan, UK	2				2			100%
Bristol, UK, City Museum and Art Gallery	4	2			2			50.0%
Brussels, Belgium, *Musée Royaux d'Art et d'Histoire*	13	3		6	3	1		69.23%
Copenhagen, Denmark, Copenhagen *Nationalmuseet*	6	2	2		2			66.67%
Copenhagen, Denmark, *Ny Carlsberg Glyptotek*	2	1			1			50.0%
Cortona, Italy, *Museo dell'Accademia*	2					2		TBD
Edinburgh, UK, National Museums of Scotland	5	2	1		2			60.0%
Exeter, UK, Royal Albert Memorial Museum	1	1						0%
Florence, Italy, *Museo Archeologico*	17	4	3	2	8			76.47%
Houston, TX, USA, Houston Museum of Natural Science	1	1						0%
Leeds, UK, City Museum	2	2						0%
Leiden, Netherlands, *Rijksmuseum van Oudheden*	13	6	3	1	3			54.0%
Liverpool, UK, World Museum, National Museums Liverpool	4		3		1			100%
London, UK, British Museum	32	16	9	1	6			50.0%
London, UK, Petrie Museum	1				1			100%
Manchester, UK	2		1				1	50.0%
New York, NY, USA, Metropolitan Museum of Art	24	7	6		9	2		62.5%
Paris, France, *Musée du Louvre*	33	10	7	8	6			63.64%
Perth, Scotland, UK	2				2			100%
Stockholm, Sweden, Stockholm *Medelhavsmuseet*	8	1	1		1	1	4	25.0%
Swansea, UK, The Wellcome Museum	1		1					100%
Turin, Italy, *Museo Egizio*	20	6	4	4	5	1		65.0%
Vatican City State, *Museo Gregoriano Egizio*	16	9	1	1	5			43.75%
Vienna, Austria, *Kunsthistorisches Museum*	19	6	4		7		2	57.89%
Warrington, UK, Warrington Museum & Art Gallery	2				2			100%
Totals	255	90	50	24	72	8	11	59.33%
Totals for reuse with high confidence				24	72			37.65%

Table 6: Coffin Reuse on all examples analysed up to 2015, by country – 255 Coffins total.

coffin, and this could very well be a mistake in the coffin production, rectified in the decoration phase. None of the other 19th Dynasty coffins have shown any evidence of reuse; that is, they were not made from a reused 18th Dynasty or earlier 19th Dynasty coffin. Once we move to the 20th Dynasty coffins, however, the evidence immediately shifts, and one example, an inner coffin in Toronto[220] with an inscription dating to the reign of Setnakht, shows a style modification from 19th Dynasty to 20th Dynasty. On this coffin,[221] plaster ears were added to what had previously been just modelled ear lobes, ostensibly to update a man's 19th Dynasty coffin that displayed the male deceased with a tiered wig with only his earlobes showing to a style in which his full ear was represented.

Thus far, I have seen about 250 coffins in person – documenting them photographically and examining them for reuse. The rate of evidence for reuse for coffins analysed thus far in the twenty-six museums I have visited stands now at about 60% (Table 6).

---

220 Royal Ontario Museum, inv. no. 910.5.1-2.
221 P. Lewin *et al.* (eds), 'Nakht: A Weaver of Thebes,' *Rotunda: The Magazine of the Royal Ontario Museum* 7, no. 4 (1974).

In other words, about 60% of the 21st to early 22nd Dynasty coffins show evidence that they were reused for another deceased individual. Even if I remove those coffins for which there is only a suspicion of reuse, the rate comes in at almost 40%. Furthermore, I suspect much of the reuse is still cleverly hidden. If I could scan underneath the plaster and easily see older plaster layers (all but impossible with current X-ray technology) or perform Carbon-14 dating of the wood and expose the reuse of old lumber, I suspect that the evidence of reuse would be much higher. Technical examinations have shown 'clean' coffins to have actually been made of reused coffin wood. The late 20th or early 21st Dynasty coffin of Nespawershefyt in Cambridge,[222] for instance, showed no obvious evidence of reuse to me in person, but a CT scan revealed older mortis joins hidden inside the carpentry of the inner coffin.[223]

My analysis is art historical in its foundation: careful in-person examination with a variety of light sources, usually a basic white light, but sometimes benefiting from infrared photography (for the area where the personal name is inscribed in particular), UV light (for examination of varnished surfaces) and, thanks to Elsbeth Geldhof's help, digital microscopy (which can show multiple layers of painted decoration if there is a break in the surface decoration). I have also performed Carbon-14 dating on a few coffins in the dataset, one example being a *stola* coffin in a private collection, now on display in the Houston Museum of Natural Science,[224] indicating that part of the coffin wood is 19th Dynasty in date, much older than the early 22nd Dynasty date of its decoration according to the accepted stylistic typologies.[225] My analysis of this Houston coffin revealed no visible evidence of reuse, but the older wood provided a circumstantial marker in favour of this practice. Another coffin in Turin (Inv. No. 2221),[226] also tested with Carbon-14 dating, reveals that the wood was many hundreds of years older than the late 21st Dynasty style, too great a difference to be explained away by ancient oversized trees.[227] Both the Houston and Turin coffins were made of native Egyptian woods, probably acacia and sycamore fig, respectively, and were probably made of timber cut from much smaller trees than a centuries-old cedar from the Lebanon. In other words, I suspect that if Carbon-14 could be applied to the entire dataset, then the rate of funerary reuse from mid-20th Dynasty to early 22nd Dynasty would again be much higher than 60%.

6.2 Methodology

In Table 6 above, I have graded my own confidence in the evidence for coffin reuse from 0 to 3, 0 being the number assigned to coffins with no evidence of reuse, 1 the number assigned when only circumstantial evidence can be found, 2 the assigned number when there is stronger evidence, and 3 when there is obvious and conclusive proof of reuse on a given coffin. As my research has developed, I have also included a 0.5 when there is just

---

222 Cambridge inv. no. E.1.1822, cf. e.g. Niwiński, *21st Dynasty Coffins*, pp. 133-134, no. 56.
223 H. Strudwick and J. Dawson, *Death on the Nile: Uncovering the Afterlife of Ancient Egypt*, London 2016, pp. 182-189, #26.
224 J.P. Maclean, *The Archaeological Collection of the Western Reserve Historical Society*, Cleveland 1901.
225 Some of the wood used for the Houston coffin lid (4 samples) is significantly younger than 950 BCE, dating to early 22nd Dynasty, on point with the *stola* coffin decoration and indicating that Egypt was finally seeing new wood cultivation after the years of scarcity during the 21st Dynasty. The coffin case, however, shows dates that are about 300 years older than those of the lid (from two different samples). Either the coffin case was made of wood from the centre (i.e. the oldest part) of a very large tree that was felled more than 300 years earlier, or it is recycled wood. The latter explanation is the likeliest, given that this wood was native. Thanks to John Southon of University of California at Irvine who conducted the carbon dating.
226 A. Fabretti, F. Rossi, and R. Lanzone, *Regio Museo Di Torino: Antichità Egizie*, Turin 1882, p. 301.
227 The calibrated Carbon-14 dates come in at 1687-1611 BCE for a sample from the lid's left side and 1917-1865 BCE for a sample from the case's right side. Thanks to John Southon of University of California at Irvine who conducted the carbon dating.

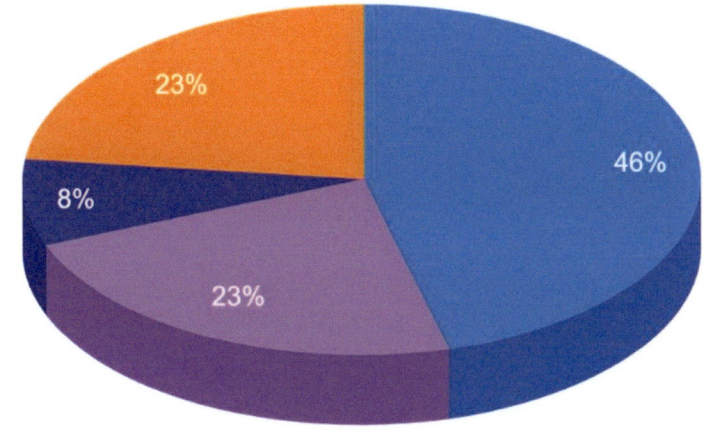
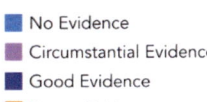

Figure 40: Leiden Coffins: Evidence for Reuse.

a bare suspicion of reuse, when the evidence is not strong enough for even a score of 1. The number on the bottom right shows that approximately 55% of the coffins examined thus far show reuse, a much higher proportion than I envisioned when I set out to find the lost Ramesside coffins seven years ago.[228]

In June 2012, I examined all yellow coffins currently in the *Rijksmuseum van Oudheden* in Leiden, in order to elucidate different methods of reuse. I excluded most fragments, preferring to look at complete pieces. The results from the *Rijksmuseum van Oudheden* actually showed significant markers of coffin reuse. Seven out of 13 coffins in Leiden showed evidence of reuse, but of those, only four of them showed strong evidence. In all, about 54% of the available coffins in the *Rijksmuseum van Oudheden* showed reuse, which is in line with the overall rate of 57%.

The reasons for this high rate of reuse are many. First, we are dealing with a time period of economic scarcity, and while pigment and varnish seems to have been available to Theban elites, wood was a limited commodity. It is highly likely that the only way to procure a transformative coffin for the one's loved one was by reusing a coffin from the family tomb RO by buying a reused coffin at a craft installation of some kind. Second, many of the Leiden coffins find their origin in the *Bab el-Gasus* cache, which I have found has higher evidence of reuse than the 21st Dynasty coffin assemblage as a whole. Long story short: when faced with scarcity, the only moral solution for the ancient Egyptians was to take their ancestors out of their coffins, bring these coffins to a craft workshop for redecoration, ideally updating the coffin style and adding the name and title of the new deceased individual to be contained in the object.

As for Leiden's 21st and early 22nd Dynasty coffins, the reuse evidence is on target with the larger dataset. About 54% of the coffins show some evidence of reuse, 23% of those with very strong evidence.

Identifying coffin reuse is a challenging business and includes finding pigments under plaster layers and paint under varnish layers, or by observing inconsistency between a coffin's poor quality decoration and the fine quality wood from which it was built from. This article will, I hope, elucidate what evidence for reuse can look like, from the most obvious examples to the most circumstantial, giving other researchers a chance to correct and supplement my work. Despite my subjective eye, it is my hope that this research will provide a better idea of how the Egyptians covered their tracks when they were reusing a coffin and what they felt was absolutely necessary to change when using the coffin again for a new occupant.

---

228 I will work with the 21st Dynasty coffins in the Royal Cache from Deir el Bahari (tomb DB 320) in December of 2016.

By the same token, I realised that our current 21st Dynasty coffin typology[229] was needlessly complicated, precisely *because* of reuse – because craftsmen often took shortcuts, keeping older elements, only updating what was really necessary. Thus, a given coffin might have a 19th Dynasty wig style but a mid-20th Dynasty collar and pectoral, or 19th Dynasty modelled feet and 20th Dynasty yellow background decoration. The practice of coffin reuse results in a mélange of styles, making typological seriation a complicated endeavour.

Even though he was the first to suggest that most Ramesside coffins were reused in the ensuing dynasties, Niwiński rarely saw reuse clearly in the coffin record. Ironically, instead of identifying the reuse visible on a given coffin, Niwiński often concluded that what he was seeing represented archaism instead and that the Egyptians were referring back to earlier fashions.[230] Perhaps it was because I wrote my first book on 19th and 20th Dynasty coffins, but I am often able to see older decoration styles and modelling, even in fragmentary form, as just that – evidence of older coffins. For example, if a 21st Dynasty coffin has a wig that was out of fashion by that point in time and more in line with a 19th Dynasty type coffin, then I am more liable to conclude that this coffin was reused and that the craftsman retained the older wig.

The data will be analysed according to set. If a coffin and mummy board were found together, they are analysed here together as a set, with the knowledge that some coffins may have been put together by dealers, rather than by the ancient funerary specialists.

---

229 This typology is based on Niwiński, *21st Dynasty Coffins*. For more discussion of 21st Dynasty coffin typologies, see R. van Walsem, 'The Study of 21st Dynasty Coffins from Thebes', *Bibliotheca Orientalis* 50 (1993), pp. 9-91; Cooney, New Typology of 21st Dynasty Coffins.

230 For example, the inner coffin of Tamutmutef (Turin inv. nos. 2228, CG 10119a-b, 10120) has a lid with the female deceased holding one arm bent against her chests and the other flat on her thigh, while the contours of her body are carved out of the surface wood. Niwiński, *21st Dynasty Coffins*, p. 172 dated this coffin to the late 21st Dynasty in his catalogue, while I see the coffin as a reused 19th Dynasty female coffin type that once showed the deceased female in daily dress, with arms holding ivy or convulvus leaves, repainted with a yellow Osirian decoration typical of the 21st Dynasty (see K.M. Cooney, 'Changing Burial Practices at the End of the New Kingdom: Defensive Adaptations in Tomb Commissions, Coffin Commissions, Coffin Decoration, and Mummification,' *Journal of the American Research Center in Egypt* 47 (2011), pp. 34-36). Indeed, Niwiński, *21st Dynasty Coffins*, creates a new type – Type Ivc – for female owners of this type of coffin, seeing it as archaizing (pp. 79-80). I feel it is safer to see this not as an archaizing type, but as an opportunistic reuse of an older style when craftsmen are taking shortcuts and not redoing a coffin completely.

6.3 Coffin data from The *Rijksmuseum van Oudheden*

Leiden inv. no. AH 1a – Nsypanebiawib – Mummy Board – No Evidence of Reuse (Fig. 41)

This early 21st Dynasty mummy board belonged to a male official. It has no visible signs of reuse. There is careful carving of face and ears with a minimum of plaster as well as attentive draftsmanship on the face using a red line in eye lid, lips, ears, neck. The ultraviolet light shows orpiment and original varnish surface.

Figure 41: AH 1a Mummy Board. Photo: Remy Hiramoto.

Leiden inv. no. AH 188 – Penpi – Mummy Board – No Evidence of Reuse (Fig. 42)

This *stola* mummy board of a man dates to the early 22nd Dynasty and includes a great deal of text. There are signs of reuse. The plaster relief on the board's surface is skilfully done. In the larger Theban dataset, *stola* coffins rarely show any signs of decorative reuse, that is, of an older coffin having been scraped of their decoration and redecorated. Van Walsem pointed out that *stola* coffins all have narrower proportions than earlier 21st Dynasty coffins, suggesting to me that if *stola* coffins were reused, they were made of broken-down reused coffin wood. The C-14 dates from the Houston coffin, cited above, corroborate the suspicion that *stola* coffins were often made of older wood, suggesting that they were made of wood from reused coffins, even if there are no obvious signs of reuse.

Figure 42: AH 188 Mummy Board 2. Photo: Meryl King.

Leiden inv. no. AMM 18-g – Ankhefenkhonsu – Outer Set – No Evidence of Reuse (Fig. 43)

This outer and inner *stola* coffin set shows no signs of reuse, as expected with coffins of this type (see above AH 188).

Figure 43: AMM 18-g Outer Coffin. Photo: Neil Crawford.

Leiden inv. no. F 93/10.1a – Gautseshen – Outer Coffin – Strong Evidence of Reuse (Figs 12 and 44)

This late 21st Dynasty coffin set from *Bab el-Gasus* is a complete one, with inner and outer coffin, and mummy board. I will treat each piece individually.

The outer coffin shows circumstantial evidence of reuse. It was made for a woman, but the two-dimensional figures on the lower part of the coffin lid show only a man, either mummiform or as an *akh*, giving offerings to divinities. It is possible that the hands and breasts were changed from male to female, but more analysis is needed. When coffins are badly restored, as in the Leiden coffins, additional materials are added that cover over seams and cracks. Modern materials have obscured my view of the stratigraphy, and I cannot tell if the hands and breasts were changed unless a thorough removal of the modern fill material is undertaken. Having said that, I nonetheless observe on this piece that plaster patches were added to balance the woman's hands after some kind of modification, suggesting a craft change from male fisted hands to female flat hands.

I originally thought that the name of Gautseshen on the lid's feet was added in another scribal hand, but it appears now to have been inscribed in the same polychrome paint, according to my visual inspection after the coffin was cleaned. Further testing is required to determine if the pigment of the name belongs to the same stratigraphy as the rest of the text. The name was painted in a rougher manner than the rest of the surrounding text, suggesting that another, later, scribal hand other than the one that had decorated the coffin had inscribed the name. Poor quality of inscription is not enough to prove a later inscription, however, and it would be wise to do a material and stratigraphic analysis of this area. Interestingly, there are blank spaces for the woman's name on the case sides of the outer and inner coffins that have never been filled in. Ostensibly, the new name (after old names were presumably removed) was never written here; It is unclear why craftsmen decided not to inscribe the name of the deceased in all the appropriate coffin locations, but the lacking inscriptions could indicate either an incomplete name reuse or a double reuse.

The seam finishes of the lid and case of the outer coffin do not match. The case has ledges, while the lid has flat seams. Coffins of the 18th and 19th Dynasty were usually ledged to fit one another. As reuse became more prevalent, it seems to have been common practice to craft a new lid with flat seams for an older case that retained its older ledges.

There is evidence of gilding at neck, and there are also specks of gold at the wrists. The title and names are for a woman, and the checkerboard wig is for a woman. There is no trace of another paint layer underneath the current wig layer, even where plaster is broken. In fact, there is no trace of older decoration anywhere under the surface of the current plaster layer.

The lids of both pieces show notches between the feet, modelled legs with a deep depression between them, as a Ramesside piece might have, however there is not any evidence of modelled wooden arms beyond the elbows. This lack of modelling, in combination with a flat seam, indicates that the outer coffin lid was ostensibly carpentered later in the 21st Dynasty.

Figure 44: F 93/10.1a Outer Coffin. Photo: Neil Crawford.

Figure 45: F 93/10.1b Inner Coffin. Photo: Meryl King.

Leiden inv. no. F 93/10.1b – Anonymous – Inner Coffin in Coffin Set of Gautseshen – Good Evidence of Reuse (Figs 13 and 45)

The cases of this inner and the above mentioned outer coffin are very close in style and iconography. The two dimensional figures have a similar style. The inner and outer coffin also have the same *tit* and cobra frieze in high relief repeated on the case upper surface. (Coffins often have a frieze of symbols along the upper and lower horizontal lines of decoration.) The inner coffin also has a similar checkerboard wig and similar collar decoration as the outer piece. Both inner and outer coffin cases have a very thin layer of plaster with no previous decoration visible underneath. Elsbeth Geldhof's analysis revealed the same ochre and orpiment layer on as background colour for all the body containers in the set.

The seams of the lid and case do not match; the lid has flat seams while the case has lodged. The piece is likely reused simply because the seams do not match.

The inner coffin has no preserved name at all. The side seams have remnants of the title *nbt pr šmʿyt n ʾImn-rʿ* (mistress of the House, chantress of Amun-Re), but the name of Gautseshen is missing because the feet of the coffin have broken off. This title is generically feminine and was probably inscribed for Gautseshen's reuse of the inner coffin, along with her now missing name.

Just like the outer coffin, there is no evidence of any decorative reuse. The inner coffin face was stolen, possibly because of its gilded surface. There are still remnants of gilding visible at the neck. One of the hands is gone, but the remaining hand is not gilded, so here the idea that a thief tempted by gold and might have stolen it is less plausible. Yet the lost hand is a further indication for a gender reuse on this coffin set. Keeping the gilded face but change the hands into a non-gilded female version, would have been the easiest modification to turn a male's coffin into a female's one.

There are no traces of old modelling underneath the current plaster layer. No prior decoration, just native wood and plaster visible.

Leiden inv. no. F 93/10.1c – Anonymous – Mummy Board in Coffin Set of Gautseshen – Circumstantial Evidence of Reuse (Figs 14 and 46)

Like the other pieces in the set associated with Gautseshen in the museum records, the entire surface of the mummy board has a layer of yellow ochre and orpiment. Interestingly, the mummy board has no inscription whatsoever, for a name or otherwise, and there is no indication that there was ever any intention to include text.

It had a gilded face that is now gone. There are traces of gilding around the neck. Like the outer coffin, the hands are not gilded, a sign of gender modification and reuse because a coffin with a gilded face would ostensibly been made with matching gilded hands. The hands are painted with red lines. The decoration on the mummy board matches the outer pieces, with the same tit and cobra frieze in high relief is repeated on its surface, but, unlike the outer and inner coffin, there is a tremendous amount of raised plaster relief with no trace of text anywhere on the piece. Perhaps the earlier paint was removed from the mummy board, but the plaster relief was not? In any case, the decorative style – flat vs. raised plaster relief – do not match from coffin to mummy board as we would expect in Egyptian coffins of the yellow type.[231] The mummy board has a long collar, as typical for later 21st Dynasty coffins and, as such, it is likely a later redecoration. It has a checked headdress and breasts both of which match the inner and outer coffins, also likely later redecorations.

The mummy board shows no traces of decorative reuse, but the head does show an overlapping structural piece, more akin to an earlier 19th or 20th Dynasty mummy board.

There are only circumstantial signs of reuse: including a gilded face but only painted hands; plaster relief that doesn't match the other pieces in the set.

Without stratigraphic analysis of the pigments or other material analysis, I can't be sure when the individual pieces were originally created and if they were created for a unified coffin set, but they were at some point inner coffin, outer coffin, and mummy board were all redecorated to match for this one coffin set.

---

231 See my work on Ramesside coffins, for example, in which inner coffins with plaster relief almost always have mummy boards with the same plaster relief. See "Group 2" in Cooney, *Cost of Death*, pp. 404-418.

Figure 46: F 93/10.1c Mummy Board. Photo: Meryl King.

Leiden inv. no. F 93/10.2a – Nesytanebtawy – Outer Coffin – Strong Evidence of Reuse (Figs 15 and 47)

This late 21st Dynasty *Bab el-Gasus* outer coffin once belonged to a woman called Nesytanebtawy, but was, without much care or attention, turned into the coffin set of a man. The artisan added blue stripes to the already varnished female wig without removing any of the original decoration, a feature noted with the naked eye, but investigated stratigraphically by conservator Elsbeth Geldhof who was able to determine that the later paint layer was added directly to the varnished surface. The previous female blue wig is still visible underneath. The artisans also did not remove the woman's original name and titles from the case sides or from the bottom of the feet of the outer coffin. The varnished breasts were also retained and are clearly visible, and for the transformation into a man's coffin, they were simply covered with blue paint. Interestingly, artisans added a blue or green chin strap to the face, applied over the varnish, to further masculinise it. There is also the trace of a small hole under the chin, very small, maybe for a beard hole. In the end, this outer coffin betrays potential multiple reuse, including decorative reuse of the upper body, and gender modification that altered the headdress, hands, and breasts.

If the artisans did such a poor job of making this originally female's outer coffin into a man's, then perhaps it demonstrates that the focus of ritual transformation was on the inner coffin, not on the outer coffin.[232] Interestingly, this outer coffin is almost certainly a double reuse because the case has a stepped seam edge, while the coffin lid has a flat seam edge, indicating that the two pieces were not made for one another. The lid was ostensibly constructed at a later date than the case for a female; then the lid and case were opportunistically brought together to craft a coffin that was redone for a man, while keeping the case largely as it was.

---

232 For a similar idea for 19th Dynasty coffins, see Cooney, *Cost of Death*, Chapter 7.

Figure 47 : F 93/10.2a Outer Coffin. Photo: Neil Crawford.

Figure 48: F 93/10.2b Inner Coffin. Photo: Neil Crawford.

Leiden inv. no. F 93/10.2b – Anonymous Man – Inner Coffin – Circumstantial Evidence of Reuse (Figs 16 and 48)

This late 21st Dynasty *Bab el-Gasus* inner coffin came to the museum as a set belonging to Nesytanebtawy. We have seen above that her outer coffin above that was later made into a man's (F 93/10.2a) and we will see below that it was only at that time equipped with a mummy board (indeed also of a man (F 93/10.2c)). In fact, there was never any name inscribed anywhere on the inner coffin. The plaster all around the masculine fisted hands is indicative of gender modification and thus reuse, but more technical studies of the plaster layers – stratigraphic analysis of paint and plaster to see if there are multiple plastered surfaces on the coffin – need to be done to make any definitive statements. Another circumstantial marker in favour of reuse of Nesytanebtawy's inner coffin for a man at some point is the fact that there is also a thin strap painted under the chin, applied over the varnish of the face, of the same kind and colour as the chin strap painted onto the outer coffin.[233] This inner coffin also has a blank where the deceased's name should be at the end of the offering list along the seam of the inner coffin's case left. In addition, like the outer coffin, the inner coffin also has seams that don't match, showing a lid with flat seams and a case with ledged seams, suggesting that the two parts of the inner body container were not made for one another.

A closer look at the coffin's hands brings up some other interesting details. Artisans added generous amounts of plaster to the surface of the wooden hands and to every seam where the hands joins with the coffin, creating a smooth layer to which red paint lines have been added to differentiate fingers. I have seen this craft technique frequently, not only on later 21st Dynasty lids, but also on coffins that have other markers of reuse. Plaster is one of the favourite tools of the artisans performing reuse. Having said all of this, the coffin lid's left fist has come away from the plaster surface, and there is no trace of any older decoration underneath betraying an original flat female hand. If a female hand had been there, it is likely that the original and longer outline of the flat hand would have been visible in the plaster outline and surrounding painted decoration.

A close examination of the upper body showed that the paint layers making up the headdress, collar, and lower body decoration all seem contemporary as one decorative layer adapted for Nesytanebtawy, albeit over thick layers of plaster that suggests a previous decoration layer, even though here is no visible evidence of older decoration.

When the outer and inner coffins are compared, the outline hand and layout seem different, suggesting that the pieces were brought together opportunistically and were not originally crafted to be a coffin set. The outer coffin has finer and more carefully applied decoration at the feet, and space for the addition of a title and name. The inner coffin has only rough patterning at the bottom of the feet and no space for a name. Such differences in quality and layout would not be likely in a yellow coffin set decorated to match.[234]

The blank for the name provides interesting details because it seems the artisans were careless in removing text for the new name within an offering list, instead of in the kind of text where the name should appear. The standard offering formula lists 1000 of bread, beer, beef, fowl, etc., with the number followed by the preposition *m* [of] and then the specific offering type. The reusing artisans created a blank for the new owner's name after one of these m prepositions, misunderstanding the sense of the sentence written on the side of the coffin. In other words, a blank space was created to name a new coffin owner, but it wasn't put in the correct place in the text.

---

233 A chin strap is indicative of a false beard, a facial adornment worn by men, not women.

234 Cooney, *Cost of Death*, pp. 194-197; pp. 213-218.

Figure 49: F 93/10.2c Mummy board. Photo: Meryl King.

Leiden inv. no. F 93/10.2c – Anonymous – Mummy Board – No Evidence of Reuse (Figs 17 and 49)

This late 21st Dynasty *Bab el-Gasus* mummy board came to Leiden in the same set as the above inner and outer coffin associated to Nesytanebtawy. It was decorated without any intention of attaching names and titles. The feet have no vertical text inscriptions, only pattern blocking. The mummy board has no hands, which is strange for a 21st Dynasty piece and might be indicative of a cheaper production of a board or a very late piece, perhaps early 22nd Dynasty when the inclusion of hands started to go out of fashion.[235] It is also a copy of a finer *stola* type.

There are very circumstantial markers of reuse, including a summarily carved face with very thick mud and finishing plaster applied to fill it out. This technique is quite common on non-*stola* coffins constructed later in the 21st and early 22nd Dynasties. Otherwise, the surface is clean with no evidence of reuse of any kind. Elsbeth Geldhof examined the piece with raking light and also saw no modifications or inconsistencies. The plaster is thin, and any breaks show only wood underneath. It would be interesting to perform Carbon-14 dating on the wood used to make this mummy board to determine if it is older or younger wood. The beard may or may not have originally been attached to this coffin, as it seems too large for the mummy board. Might it have been added by a dealer instead?

---

235 See Niwiński, *21st Dynasty Coffins*, pp. 81-82.

Leiden inv. no. F 93/10.3a – Anonymous – Inner Coffin – Strong Evidence of Reuse (Figs 18 and 50)

The first sign of reuse on this late 21st Dynasty *Bab el-Gasus* coffin is the fact that the entire surface is very rough, as if it has been chiselled of the old decoration for a new layer. The surface decoration shows a woman, although strangely, the earrings, which had been created out of plaster, have been knocked off and painted over. This inner coffin was associated with the coffin set Tentpenheroenefer, but no name was ever inscribed on the coffin. A reuse is indicated by a hieratic text naming a wꜥb-priest of Amun, Khonsuiry,[236] was inscribed on the underside of the feet. Ostensibly, the last coffin owner Tentpenheroenefer was removed for this priest, even though few decorative changes were performed on the coffin, only the rough addition of a cursive name on the bottom of the feet to mark the reusing owner's identity and a few quick modifications to change the gender of the coffin to masculine.

Given the hieratic text naming a man, a closer look reveals a very summary gender modification. The plaster earrings were knocked off and covered with a thin layer of blue paint, and ears were drawn in red paint onto the surface of the headdress. No other modifications of breasts and hands were attempted on this inner coffin. The same treatment is seen on the mummy board – the same blue paint over the earrings, red paint for the ears, and the same non-removal of breasts and hands.

There are no signs of varnish on this inner coffin, only yellow paint, which seems to be a mix of ochre and yellow orpiment. The coffin case was decorated for a woman, like the lid, and a picture of a woman is shown in the painted coffin decoration offering and worshipping in numerous scenes. There was very little text inscribed overall on this coffin, evidence that supports the fact that a name was never inscribed.

The lid has flat seam edges, while the case for the coffin has a ledged seam edges, indicating that there may be a previous reuse for the coffin before the gender modification.

The earrings used to be red and yellow with varnish, on both the coffin (and mummy board). And the wig on the coffin (and mummy board as well) have an unusual paint layering of black under blue, suggesting that the wig treatment was the same on both pieces.

There is more circumstantial evidence of the reuse: the interior of the inner coffin shows chiselling away of the wood surface, ostensibly to fit the mummy and mummy board. Perhaps a coffin used for a woman was now being used for a man too large to fit?

---

236 Editorial note: For an alternative interpretation see p. 47 of this book.

Figure 50: F 93/10.3a Inner Coffin. Photo: Meryl King.

Leiden inv. no. F 93/10.3b – Tjenetpenherunefer – Mummy Board – Strong Evidence of Reuse (Figs 18 and 51)

This is an early 21st Dynasty mummy board, but it came to Leiden with a coffin of late 21st Dynasty style, suggesting the reuse of a very early mummy board with a very late coffin. The mummy board actually looks Ramesside in form because it has a curved shape in profile, not flat over the body, but wrapping around it somewhat, as seen in the 20th Dynasty mummy board of Nysuamen in Leeds (D.1960.426). The name was clearly added in a different hand, suggestive of reuse.

The area where the name is inscribed is rather small and the text seems cramped and messy, as if it was forced to fit. It is also possible that the varnish is of a different consistency and layering here where the names are, also indicative of modifications. As on the inner coffin, the earrings have been covered with a layer of blue paint, and ears were drawn onto the headdress in red paint. Assuming that this is a gender modification, the efforts didn't go farther than this; the craftsmen left her flat female hands. The painted decoration on the wig retains the lappet bands seen on a female headdress.

The text on the mummy board is complicated with numerous palimpsests. There are traces of a *w'b*-sign barely visible written over the 'Tjenet' part of the female name Tjenetpenherunefer, written *over* the varnish. Maybe the same *w'b*-priest Khonsuiry named in the hieratic docket on the inner coffin of Tjenetpenherunefer (see above F 93/10.3b) had the mummy board re-inscribed for himself. over the varnish, i.e. reusing the whole set. Since the writing was applied over the varnish, most of that text has flaked away. The surface of the mummy board is also quite rough, and it seems to have been finished only with mud/clay plaster, not with white plaster as usual. The inscription on the mummy board reads: *jn Wsjr nbt pr šm'yt (n 'Imn) Tnt-p(n)-ḥrw-nfr ḏd=s* (Osiris, mistress of the House, chantress (of Amun), Tjenetp[en]herunefer, she says…) Between the *Wsjr* and the *ḏd=s*, there was not enough room for both the titles and a name of this length, and the craftsmen had to squeeze it into the space. This suggests yet another reuse by Tjenetpenherunefer before it was reused again for Khonsuiry.

This is a complicated coffin set with 1) gender modification on all pieces, 2) added hieratic docket on the inner coffin, 3) mismatched case and lid of inner coffin, 4) mismatching inner coffin and mummy board. The coffin and mummy board came to Leiden as a set, but while the coffin is much later in style than the mummy board and while the coffin was left unvarnished while the mummy board was varnished, the artisan's hand that drew the ears on both mummy board and coffin seems the same. Thus, it seems that although the two pieces were originally made for different sets, they were reused together at some point in the later 21st or early 22nd Dynasties.

Figure 51: F 93/10.3b Mummy Board. Photo: Meryl King.

Leiden inv. no. AMM 18-h – Djedmonthuiuefankh – Stola, Inner Coffin – No Evidence of Reuse (Fig. 52)

This late 21ˢᵗ or early 22ⁿᵈ Dynasty *stola* coffin has a striped wig and a great deal of text in vertical blue and white columns on coffin lid. The piece is obviously well published by Van Walsem, who mentions no reuse on the coffin.²³⁷ I also see no signs of reuse.

---

237 Van Walsem, *Djedmonthuiufankh*. Van Walsem is certainly aware of coffin reuse, as he mentions other instances in his monograph on Stola coffins, but he nowhere provides any evidence that the Leiden Stola coffin of Djedmonthuiufankh was in any way reused. On p. 43, Van Walsem concludes the Stola coffins and non-Stola coffins have different proportions, the stola being narrower in shape overall than the non-Stola. I would further Van Walsem's analysis and conclude that Stola coffins would not usually show any evidence of reuse because their narrower proportions prove that they could not be made out of previous coffins. If a Stola coffin was made out of another coffin, then the older coffin was first broken down into lumber pieces and stripped of any previous decoration before using that wood again.

Figure 52: (enlarged detail on right page) AMM 18-h Djedmonthuiuefankh Stola, Inner Coffin. Photo RMO.

6.4 Conclusion

The close examination of a group of coffins for evidence of reuse is both hyper-detailed and broadly anthropological. The catalogue of evidence is necessary for other researchers to check my work and, if that is even possible, see through my eyes. Detailed conservation information is necessary so that Egyptologists know what analysis has technical examination behind it, and what is supported visual examination alone. Once all the evidence is described and analysed, however, we are left with a percentage of coffin reuse that is on point with the 21st Dynasty coffin dataset as a whole – almost 60% – and if we could examine these coffins with more technical methods, the percentage would certainly be higher. And then we are left with the surprise that there is so much evidence for a human behaviour that the Egyptians themselves never talked about in a positive way. This high percentage speaks to the time of crisis and material scarcity, yes, but it also speaks to a communal agree to that coffin reuse was the best possible way to deal with this practical problem.

In the ancient textual record, tomb robbery and funerary arts reuse were discussed either in a punitive context (as in the Tomb Robbery Papyri) when people are being interrogated and tried, or it was purposefully veiled (like in the Late Ramesside Letters or the Deir el-Medina inventory texts).[238] But the fact that almost 60% of the Leiden museum 21st Dynasty coffins were reused suggests that everyone was engaging in this practice to transform and protect their dead relatives. We just have no direct written evidence of it. But why would anyone have written down that they took a family ancestor out of her coffin, moved her mummy to a corner of the tomb, took the coffin out of the tomb, redecorated it with appropriate and fashionable decoration, and used it for another relative? This was unseemly behaviour, best kept disguised.

For most of its history, Egyptology has looked upon tomb robbery and funerary arts reuse as aberrant, regressive, and abnormal. Documents like the Tomb Robbery Papyri[239] have reinforced that mind set. In their literature, the Egyptians themselves repeatedly describe the ideal (read: 'normal') burial situation as a stone house in which the ancestors reside for eternity, supported by income-producing lands set aside in an endowment to pay for priests and provisions in perpetuity. However, in the last two decades, many Egyptologists have looked to the entire 'life cycle' of a tomb, pointing out that tomb robbery and reuse were not only a part of necropolis life, but that tomb robbery had been practiced since the beginnings of ancient Egyptian complex society, a reality of which the Egyptians themselves were well aware.[240]

The rate of reuse on these Leiden coffins allows us to understand that the ancient Egyptians saw funerary transformation as their priority. Once the dead had benefitted from the coffin materiality in ritual, both public and private, the coffin did not absolutely have to remain with the dead. This longer term agenda – perpetual ownership by the dead – was usually prohibitively expensive and only possible during times of plenty. Inevitably, times of crisis, like the 21st Dynasty – hit any civilization, and it is during these lean years that accumulated materiality can be recommodified and reused.

---

238 For discussion thereof, see K.M. Cooney, 'Placating the Dead: Evidence of Social Crisis in Three Texts from Western Thebes', in: K.M. Cooney and K.E. Davis (eds), *Joyful in Thebes: Egyptological Studies in Honor of Betsy M. Bryan*, edited by Richard Jasnow, Atlanta, Georgia 2015, pp. 79-90 and Cooney, *Journal of the American Research Center in Egypt* 47, pp. 3-44.

239 T.E. Peet, *The Great Tomb-Robberies of the Twentieth Egyptian Dynasty, Being a Critical Study with Translations and Commentaries of the Papyri in Which They Are Recorded*, 2 vols. Oxford 1930.

240 J. Baines and P. Lacovara, 'Burial and the Dead in Ancient Egyptian Society: respect, formalism, neglect,' *Journal of Social Archaeology* 2, no. 1 (2002), pp. 5-36; C. Näser, *Der Alltag des Todes. Archäologische Zeugnisse und Textquellen zu funerären Praktiken und Grabplünderung in Deir El-Medine im Neuen Reich* (PhD Dissertation Humboldt-Universität zu Berlin, 2002) and C. Näser, 'Jenseits von Theben – Objektsammlung, Inszenierung und Fragmentierung in Ägyptischen Bestattungen des Neuen Reiches', in: B. Schweizer, C. Kümmel and U. Veit (eds), *Körperinszenierung – Objektsammlung – Monumentalisierung: Totenritual Und Grabkult in Frühen Gesellschaften*, ed., Archäologische Quellen in Kulturwissenschaftlicher Perspektive, Münster 2008.

Leiden museum inventory no.	Coffin Type	Coffin Part	Dating	Provenance	Name(s) of Deceased	Title	Reuse Score	Type of Reuse
AH 1a	Mummy board		early 21st Dynasty	purchased in 1828 from the collection of J. d'Anastasy	Nsypanebiawib		0	
AH 188	Mummy board		early 22nd Dynasty	from the collection of J. d'Anastasy, purchased in 1828 presented by the Egyptian Government in 1893	Penpi		0	
AMM 18	Outer coffin	Lid + case	early 22nd Dynasty	from the collection of J.d'Anastasy, purchased in 1828	Ankhefenkhonsu		0	
AMM 18	Inner coffin	Lid + case	early 22nd Dynasty	from the collection of J.d'Anastasy, purchased in 1828	Djedmenesjwankh?		0	
F 93/10.1a	Outer coffin	Lid + case	late 21st Dynasty; mummy braces of the HP Pinudjem II	from the tomb Bab el-Gasus, found in Deir el-Bahari in 1891, presented by the Egyptian Government in 1893	Gautseshen	Chantress of Amun	3	Multiple reuse, decorative reuse, name reuse, gender modification, blank space for name
F 93/10.1b	Inner coffin	Lid + case	late 21st Dynasty; mummy braces of the HP Pinudjem II	from the tomb Bab el-Gasus, found in Deir el-Bahari in 1891, presented by the Egyptian Government in 1893	Anonymous	Chantress of Amun	2	Blank space for name
F 93/10.1c	Mummy board		late 21st Dynasty; mummy braces of the HP Pinudjem II	from the tomb Bab el-Bahari in 1891, presented by the Egyptian Government in 1893	Anonymous	Chantress of Amun	1	
F 93/10.2a	Outer coffin	Lid + case	late 21st Dynasty	from the tomb Bab el-Gasus, found in Deir el-Bahari in 1891, presented by the Egyptian Government in 1893	Nesytanebtawy	Chantress of Amun	3	Multiple reuse, decorative reuse, gender modification
F 93/10.2b	Inner coffin	Lid + case	late 21st Dynasty	from the tomb Bab el-Gasus, found in Deir el-Bahari in 1891, presented by the Egyptian Government in 1893	Anonymous man	Chantress of Amun	1	Gender modification, blank space for name
F 93/10.2c	Mummy board		late 21st Dynasty	from the tomb Bab el-Gasus, found in Deir el-Bahari in 1891, presented by the Egyptian Government in 1893	Anonymous man	Anonymous	0	
F 93/10.3a	Inner coffin	Lid + case	late 21st Dynasty	from the tomb Bab el-Gasus, found in Deir el-Bahari in 1891, presented by the Egyptian Government in 1893	Anonymous	Chantress of Amun	3	Decorative reuse, gender modification
F 93/10.3b	Mummy board		late 21st Dynasty	from the tomb Bab el-Gasus, found in Deir el-Bahari in 1891, presented by the Egyptian Government in 1893	Named for Tjenetpenherunefer or Tanetpenherunefer	Chantress of Amun	3	Name reuse, markers of Ramesside coffin
AMM 18-h	Stola, Inner coffin	Lid + case	late 21st or early 22nd Dynasty		Djedmonthuiuefankh		0	

Table 7: Appendix: 21st and 22nd Dynasty Coffin Reuse in the Rijksmuseum van Oudheden.

Bibliography

Amenta, A., 'The restoration of the coffin of Butehamon. New points for reflection from scientific investigations', in *Proceedings of the Conference Ancient Egyptian Coffins. Past-Present-Future* (Cambridge, 7-9 April 2016), (in press).

Amenta, A., 'The Vatican Coffin Project', in: E. Pischikova, J. Budka and K. Griffin (eds), *Thebes in the First Millennium BC*, Cambridge 2014, pp. 483-499.

Amenta, A., (ed.), *Vatican Coffin Project, Protocollo indagini scientifiche. Analysis Protocol.*, Rome 2013.

Amenta, A., and Guichard, H. (eds.), *Proceedings of the First Vatican Coffin Conference* (Vatican Museums, 19-22 June 2013), Rome 2017.

Aston, D.A., *Burial Assemblages of Dynasty 21-25. Chronology – Typology – Development*, Vienna 2009.

Baines, J., and Lacovara, P., 'Burial and the Dead in Ancient Egyptian Society: respect, formalism, neglect,' *Journal of Social Archaeology* 2, no. 1 (2002), p. 536.

Bayard, E., 'Les découvertes de Louqsor', *L'Illustration* 49 (1891), p. 304.

Bettum, A., 'Lot XIV from Bab el-Gasus (Sweden and Norway): The modern history of the collection and a reconstruction of the ensembles', in: R. Sousa (ed.), *Body, Cosmos and Eternity: New Research Trends in the Iconography and Symbolism of Ancient Egyptian Coffins*, Oxford 2014, pp. 167-186.

Bierbrier, M.R., *The Late New Kingdom in Egypt (c.1300-664 B.C.). A Genealogical and Chronological Investigation*, Warminster 1975.

Boeser, P.A.A., 'Levensbericht van Dr. W. Pleyte', *Handelingen en Mededeelingen van de Maatschappij der Nederlandsche Letterkunde te Leiden, over het jaar 1910-1911*, Leiden 1904. See http://www.dbnl.org/tekst/_jaa003190401_01/_jaa003190401_01_0016.php, accessed on 18 January 2017.

Bucklow, S., *The Alchemy of Paint. Art, Science and Secrets from the Middle Ages*, London 2009.

Champollion, J.-F., *Notices descriptives*, Part 2, Reprogr., Genève 1972-1973.

Cennini, C. d'Andrea, *The Craftsman's Handbook "Il Libro dell'Arte"* Translated by Daniel V. Thompson Jr, New York 1933, Dover edition 1954.

Cooney, K.M., 'Ramesside Body Containers of Wood and Cartonnage from Northern Egyptian Necropolises', in: V. Verschoor *et al.* (eds), *Festschrift for René Van Walsem*, Leiden (forthcoming).

Cooney, K.M., 'The End of New Kingdom Egypt: How Ancient Egyptian Funerary Materials Can Help Us Understand Society in Crisis', in: U. Rummel and S. Kubisch (eds), *The Ramesside Period in Egypt: Studies into Cultural and Historical Processes of the 19th and 20th Dynasties, Proceedings of the International Symposium Held at Heidelberg, 5th to 7th June, 2015*, Wiesbaden (forthcoming).

Cooney, K.M., 'Placating the Dead: Evidence of Social Crisis in Three Texts from Western Thebes', in: K.M. Cooney and K.E. Davis (eds), *Joyful in Thebes: Egyptological Studies in Honor of Betsy M. Bryan*, edited by Richard Jasnow, Atlanta, Georgia 2015, pp. 79-90.

Cooney, K.M., 'Ancient Egyptian funerary arts as social documents: social place, reuse, and working towards a new typology of 21st Dynasty coffins', in: R. Sousa (ed.), *Body, Cosmos and Eternity: New Research Trends in the Iconography and Symbolism of Ancient Egyptian Coffins*, Oxford 2014, pp. 45-66.

Cooney, K.M., 'Changing Burial Practices at the End of the New Kingdom: Defensive Adaptations in Tomb Commissions, Coffin Commissions, Coffin Decoration, and Mummification,' *Journal of the American Research Center in Egypt* 47 (2011), pp. 3-44.

Cooney, K.M., *The Cost of the Death, The Social and Economic Value of Ancient Egyptian Funerary Art in the Ramesside Period*, Leiden 2007.

Daressy, G., 'Cercueils des prètres d'Amon (Deuxième Trouvaille de Deir el Bahari)', *Annales du Service des Antiquités de l'Égypte* 8 (1907), pp. 3-38.

Daressy, G., 'Ouverture des momies provenant de la Seconde Trouvaille de Deir el-Bahari', *Annales du Service des Antiquités de l'Égypte* 4 (1903), pp. 150-160.

Daressy, G., 'Procès verbal d'ouverture de la momie n° 29707', *Annales du Service des Antiquités de l'Égypte* 3 (1902), pp. 151-154.

Daressy, G., 'Les sépultures des prètres d'Ammon à Deir el-Bahari', *Annales du Service des Antiquités de l'Égypte* 1 (1900), pp. 141-148.

Daressy, G., 'Contribution à l'étude de la XXI Dynastie Égyptienne', *Révue Archaéologique* 3 (1896), pp. 73-78.

Dautant, A., et al. 'Distribution and Current Location of the French Lot from the Bab el-Gasus Cache', Poster presentation, the First Vatican Coffin Conference, Rome, June 19-22, 2013.

Dawson J., et al, 'Egyptian coffins: Materials, Construction and Decoration', in: *Death on the Nile. Uncovering the Afterlife of Ancient Egypt*, London 2016, pp. 75-111.

Dawson W.R., and Gary, P.H.K., *Catalogue of Egyptian Antiquities in the British Museum: Mummies and Human Remains* 1, London 1968.

De Buck, A., *The Egyptian Coffin Texts*, Chicago 1935.

Dodson, A., *Afterglow of Empire. Egypt from the Fall of the New Kingdom to the Saite Renaissance*. Cairo 2012.

Dodson, A., 'The Transition between the 21st and 22nd Dynasties Revisited', in: G.P.F. Broekman et al. (eds), *The Libyan Period in Egypt*, Leiden 2009, pp. 103-111.

Dodwell, C.R., *Theophilus. The Various Arts. De Diversis Artibus. Edited and translated by C.R. Dodwell*. Oxford *Medieval Texts*, Oxford 1961.

Drenkhahn, R., 'Pinsel', in: W. Helck (ed.), *Lexikon der Ägyptologie* IV, Wiesbaden 1982, pp. 1053-1054.

Egberts, A., 'Hard Times: The Chronology of "The Report of Wenamun" Revised', *Zeitschrift für ägyptische Sprache und Altertumskunde* 125 (1998), pp. 93-108.

English Heritage, *Conservation Principles, Policies and Guidance*, 2008.

Fabretti, A., et al., *Regio Museo Di Torino: Antichità Egizie*, Turin 1882.

Frinta, M.S., 'Raised Gilded Adornment of the Cypriot Icons and the Occurrence of the Technique in the West', *Gesta* XX No.2 (1981), pp. 333-347.

Gardiner, A., 'The Gods of Thebes as Guarantors of Personal Property', *Journal of Egyptian Archaeology* 48 (1962), pp. 57-69.

Gauthier, H., *Le Livre des rois d'Égypte, Volume III*, Cairo 1915.

Gettens, R.J. and Stout, G.L., *Painting Materials. A Short Encyclopaedia* (1942), unabridged and corrected republication New York 1966.

Guichard, H., Pages-Camagna, S., and Timbart, N., 'The coffin of Tanetchedmut of the Musée du Louvre: First study and restoration for the Vatican Coffin Project', in: A. Amenta and H. Guichard (eds), *Proceedings of the First Vatican Coffin Conference (Vatican Museums, 19-22 June 2013)*, Rome 2017, pp. 169-178.

Hasselbach, H., 'Bibliografie van W. Pleyte', *Oudheidkundige Mededelingen uit het Rijksmuseum van Oudheden* 67 (1987), pp. 93-99.

Harley, R.D., *Artists' Pigments c. 1600-1835. A Study in English Documentary Sources* (second revised edition), London 1982.

Jansen-Winkeln, K., *Inschriften der Spätzeit, Teil I: Die 21, Dynastie*, Wiesbaden 2007.

Jansen-Winkeln, K., 'Relative Chronology of Dyn. 21', in: E. Hornung et al. (eds), *Ancient Egyptian Chronology*, Leiden and Boston 2006, pp. 218-233.

Jansen-Winkeln, K., 'Der thebanische "Gottesstaat"', *Orientalia* 70 (2001), pp. 153-182.

Jansen-Winkeln, K., 'Die Fremdherrschaften in Ägypten im 1. Jahrtausend v. Chr.', *Orientalia* 69 (2000), pp. 1-20.

Jansen-Winkeln, K., 'Gab es in der altägyptischen Geschichte eine feudalistische Epoche?', *Die Welt des Orients* 30 (1999), pp. 7-20.

Jansen-Winkeln, K., 'Die thebanischen Gründer der 21. Dynastie', *Göttinger Miszellen* 157 (1997), pp. 49-74.

Jansen-Winkeln, K., 'Die Plünderung der Köningsgräber des Neues Reiches', *Zeitschrift für ägyptische Sprache und Altertumskunde* 122 (1995), pp. 62-78.

Jansen-Winkeln, K., 'Der Beginn der Libyschen Herrschaft in Ägypten', *Biblische Notizen* 71 (1994), pp. 78-97.

Kakoulli, I., *Greek Painting Techniques and Materials from the fourth to the First Century BC.*, London 2009.

Kemp, B., 'Soil (including mud-brick architecture)', in: P.T. Nicholson and I. Shaw (eds), *Ancient Egyptian Materials and Technology*, Cambridge 2000, pp. 78-103.

Kitchen, K.A., *The Third Intermediate Period in Egypt (1100-650 BC)³*, Warminster 1995.

Kruchten, J.-M., *Le grand texte oraculaire de Djéhoutymose*, Brussels 1986.

Kühn, H., et al., *Reclams Handbuch der künstlerischen Techniken. Band 1: Farbmittel, Buchmalerei, Tafel- und Leinwandmalerei*, Ditzingen 1997.

Küffer A., and Siegman, R., *Unter dem Schutz der Himmelsgöttin: Ägyptische Särge, Mumien und Masken in der Schweiz*, Zürich 2007.

Lacovara P., and D´Auria, S., *The Mystery of the Albany Mummies,* Albany 2016.

Laurie, A.P., *Materials of the Painter's Craft in Europe and Egypt From Earliest Times to the End of the XVIIIth Century, With Some Account of their Preparation and Use,* London 1910.

Leahy, A., 'The Libyan Period in Egypt: An Essay in Interpretation', *Libyan Studies* 16 (1985), pp. 51-65.

Lewin, P., et al. (eds), 'Nakht: A Weaver of Thebes,' *Rotunda: The Magazine of the Royal Ontario Museum* 7, no. 4 (1974).

Lipinska, J., 'Bab el-Gusus: Cache-tomb of the priests & priestesses of Amen', *KMT* 4 (1993-1994), pp. 48-60.

Looyen A.A., *Jaarboek van de Maatschappij der Nederlandse Letterkunde* 1911, pp. 127-128. (See http://www.dbnl.org/tekst/_jaa003190401_01/_jaa003190401_01_0016.php, accessed on 17 March 2017).

Maclean, J.P., *The Archaeological Collection of the Western Reserve Historical Society*, Cleveland 1901.

Mann, L., 'The Letters of Willem Pleyte', in: A. Amenta and H. Guichard (eds), *Proceedings of the First Vatican Coffin Conference*, Rome 2017, pp. 289-292.

Maspero, G., 'Les Momies royales de Déir el Bahari', *Mémoires publiés par les membres de la mission archéologique française au Caire* 1, Cairo 1889, pp. 704-706.

Maspero, G., 'Notes sur quelques points de Grammaire et d'Histoire', *Zeitschrift für ägyptische Sprache und Altertumskunde* 21 (1883), pp. 62-79.

Miller, E., 'Painterly Technique', in: A. Middleton and K. Uprichard (eds), *The Nebamun Wall Paintings. Conservation, Scientific Analysis and Display at the British Museum,* London 2008, pp. 61-67.

Montet, P., *La nécropole royale de Tanis II: Les constructions et le tombeau de Psousennes à Tanis*, Paris 1951.

Näser, C., 'Jenseits von Theben – Objektsammlung, Inszenierung und Fragmentierung in Ägyptischen Bestattungen des Neuen Reiches', in: B. Schweizer, C. Kümmel and U. Veit (eds), *Körperinszenierung – Objektsammlung – Monumentalisierung: Totenritual und Grabkult in Frühen Gesellschaften, Archäologische Quellen in Kulturwissenschaftlicher Perspektive*, Münster 2008, pp. 445-472.

Näser, C., *Der Alltag des Todes. Archäologische Zeugnisse und Textquellen zu funerären Praktiken und Grabplünderung in Deir El-Medine im Neuen Reich* (PhD Dissertation Humboldt-Universität zu Berlin, 2002).

Naguib, S.-A., *Le Clergé Féminin d'Amon Thébain à la 21e Dynastie,* Leuven 1990.

Niwiński, A., *21st Dynasty Coffins from Thebes: Chronological and Typological Studies*, Mainz 1988.

Niwiński, A., 'The Bab el-Gasus Tomb and the Royal Cache in Deir el-Bahri', *Journal of Egyptian Archaeology* 70 (1984), pp. 73-80.

Ogden, J., 'Metals', in: P.T. Nicholson and I. Shaw (eds), *Ancient Egyptian Materials and Technology*, Cambridge 2000, pp. 148-176.

Orsenigo, C., 'Turning Points in Egyptian Archaeology (1850-1950)', in: P. Piacentini (ed.), *Egypt and the Pharaohs: From the Sand to the Library – Pharaonic Egypt in the Archives and Libraries of the Università degli Studi di Milano*, Milan 2010, pp. 162-172.

Pagès-Camagna, S., 'Les matériaux au peintre: du contour au remplissage', in: G. Andreu-Lanoë et al. (eds), *L'art du Contour: Le dessin dans l'Egypte ancienne*, Paris 2013, pp. 74-81.

Payraudeau, F., 'De nouvelles annales sacerdotales de Siamon, Psousennès II et Osorkon Ier', *Bulletin de l'Institut Français d'Archéologie Orientale* 108 (2008), pp. 293-308.

Peet, T.E., *The Great Tomb-Robberies of the Twentieth Egyptian Dynasty, Being a Critical Study with Translations and Commentaries of the Papyri in Which They Are Recorded* (2 vols.), Oxford 1930.

Prestipino, G., Santamaria, U. and Morresi F., et al., 'Sperimentazione di adesivi e consolidanti per il restauro di manufatti lignei policromi egizi', in: *Lo Stato dell'Arte 13. Atti del XIII Congresso Nazionale IGIIC (Torino, 22-24 ottobre 205)*, Turin 2015, pp. 261-270.

Reeves, N., *Valley of the Kings. The Decline of a Royal Necropolis*, London 1990.

Ritner, R., 'Fragmentation and Reintegration in the Third Intermediate Period', in: G.P.F. Broekman et al. (eds), *The Libyan Period in Egypt. Historical and Cultural Studies into the 21st -24th Dynasties: Proceedings of a Conference at Leiden University, 25-27 October 2007*, Leiden and Leuven 2009, pp. 327-340.

Scott, D.A., 'A review of ancient Egyptian pigments and cosmetics', *Studies in Conservation* 61 (July 2016), pp. 185-202.

Serpico, M., and White, R., 'The Use and Identification of Varnish on New Kingdom Funerary Equipment', in: W.V. Davies (ed.), *Colour and Painting in Ancient Egypt*, London 2001, pp. 33-42.

Serpico, M., with a contribution by R. White, 'Resins, amber and bitumen', in: P.T. Nicholson and I. Shaw (eds), *Ancient Egyptian Materials and Technology*, Cambridge 2000, pp. 430-474.

Smith, E., 'An account of the mummy of a priestess of Amen supposed to be Ta-usert-em-suten-pa', *Annales du Service des Antiquités de l'Égypte* 7 (1906), pp. 155-160.

Smith, E., 'Report on the four mummies', *Annales du Service des Antiquités de l'Égypte* 4 (1903), pp. 156-160.

Sousa, R., 'Spread your wings over me: Iconography, symbolism and meaning of the central panel on yellow coffins', in: R. Sousa (ed.), *Body, Cosmos and Eternity: New Research Trends in the Iconography and Symbolism of Ancient Egyptian Coffins*, Oxford 2014, pp. 197-203.

Sousa, R., 'O Portal dos Sacerdotes: Uma leitura compreensiva do espólio de Bab el-Gassus', *Cadmo* 21 (2011), pp. 79-100.

Stacey, R., 'Paint media and varnishes', in: A. Middleton and K. Uprichard (eds), *The Nebamun Wall Paintings. Conservation, Scientific Analysis and Display at the British Museum*, London 2008, pp. 51-60.

Sternberg-el Hotabi, H., 'Die Stele der Verbannten', in: *Texte aus der Umwelt des Alten Testaments* II/1, Gütersloh 1986, pp. 112-116.

Strudwick, H. and Dawson, J., Catalogue entry '26: Coffin set of Nespawershefyt', in: J. Dawson et al, 'Egyptian Coffins: Materials, Construction and Decoration', in: *Death on the Nile. Uncovering the Afterlife of Ancient Egypt*, London 2016, pp. 182-189.

Strudwick H., and Dawson, J., *Death on the Nile: Uncovering the Afterlife of Ancient Egypt*, London 2016.

Tarasenko, M., 'The Third Intermediate Period coffins in the museums of Ukraine', A. Amenta (ed.), *First Vatican Coffin Conference, 19-22 June, 2013. Proceedings*, Vatican, Rome 2017, pp. 529-540.

Taylor, J.H., *Mummies. Death and the Afterlife in Ancient Egypt. Treasures from the British Museum*, Santa Ana 2005.

Taylor, J.H., 'Aspects of the History of the Valley of the Kings in the Third Intermediate Period', in: N. Reeves (ed.), *After Tut`Ankhamun. Research and Excavation in the Royal Necropolis at Thebes*, London 1992, pp. 186-206.

The Epigraphic Survey, *The Temple of Khonsu – Volume I, Scenes of King Herihor in the Court, Oriental Institute Publications* 100, Chicago 1979.

Vasari, G., *Vasari On Technique. Being the Introduction to the Three Arts of Design, Architecture, Sculpture, and Painting, Prefixed to the Lives of the Most Excellent Painters, Sculptors and Architects* (translated into English by Louisa S. Maclehose), London 1907.

Walsem, R. van, *The Coffin of Djedmonthuiufankh in the National Museum of Antiquities at Leiden*, Leiden 1997.

Walsem, R. van, 'The Study of 21st Dynasty Coffins from Thebes,' *Bibliotheca Orientalis* 50 (1993), pp. 9-91.

Weeks, K., *The Lost Tomb: The Greatest Discovery at the Valley of the Kings Since Tutankhamun*, London 1999.

Yoyotte, J., 'Un Pharaon Oublié?', *Bulletin de la Société française d'Égyptologie* 77-78 (1976/77), pp. 39-54.

Yoyotte, J., 'Tanis', in: J.-L. de Cénival and J. Yoyotte (eds), *Tanis, L'or des Pharaons*, Paris 1987, p. 48.